What people are saying about

Pantheon - The Norse

Morgan Daimler's new addition to the *Pantheon* series .⌐ ⌐.⌐
perfect introduction for those wishing to explore the rich
religious landscape of the Norse tradition. Like Odin's eight-
legged stead, Sleipnir, Daimler carries readers across the many
realms of Norse religious belief and practice, paying visits to
the numerous Gods and spirits who populate the nine worlds
of Norse cosmology. This book strikes the balance between
providing a concise overview for new-comers to Norse Paganism
and offering intriguing insights that invite readers to delve in
deeper. As such, this is an accessible and well-informed guide
which will appeal to those seeking to learn more about the Norse
tradition.

Olivia Church, author of *Isis: Great of Magic, She of 10,000 Names*

It can be hard for newcomers to find their footing in modern
Heathenry! The learning curve is steep and it can be all too easy
for a new Heathen to inadvertently step on one of the many
fault lines in modern Heathen communities. In *Pantheon - The
Norse*, Morgan Daimler boils down key concepts in a balanced
and nuanced way, providing both a solid overview of modern
Heathenry as well as insider knowledge for the newcomer to
help them avoid the most troublesome fault lines.

Cat Heath, author of *Elves, Witches and Gods: Spinning Old
Heathen Magic in the Modern Day*

Pantheon - The Norse by Morgan Daimler is far more than just a
simple list of gods and goddesses. Well-researched and clearly
worded, as we have come to expect from Daimler, this book
offers a comprehensive entry into the world of modern Norse

Paganism in its many varieties. Drawing on vital primary source documents, easy-to-understand explanations of the mythos, cosmology, and worldview provide the necessary background for the information about ancient and modern ritual practices, values, and manners. Then follows an insightful dive into the Aesir, Vanir, Giants, and other spirits and beings associated with the Norse traditions, some of whom the reader may find new and fascinating. The suggested reading list and extensive bibliography offer the reader a helpful way to continue their exploration. Altogether, *Pantheon - The Norse* is a thorough introduction and a valuable resource for anyone who is interested in exploring and practicing modern Norse Paganism.
Laura Perry, author of *Ariadne's Thread: Awakening the Wonders of the Ancient Minoans in Our Modern Lives*

Pantheon - the Norse by Morgan Daimler is the book I wished I had when I was first meeting the Norse gods. Not only does this serve to bring a foundation to the reader, but the balance between personal experience and academic sources helps it feel welcoming to someone beginning to explore this pantheon. It's amazing how Daimler brought together so many resources and magic in a way that is inviting and accessible. Highly recommended and highly enjoyable.
Irisanya Moon, author of *Reclaiming Witchcraft*, *Aphrodite* and *Iris*

Pantheon
The Norse

Norse Titles from Morgan Daimler

Odin
Meeting the Norse Allfather

978-1-78535-480-9 (Paperback)
978-1-78535-481-6 (e-book)

Thor
*Mythology and modern lore surrounding the
most popular Norse deity*

978-1-78904-115-6 (Paperback)
978-1-78904-116-3 (e-book)

Pantheon
The Norse

Morgan Daimler

MOON BOOKS

Winchester, UK
Washington, USA

JOHN HUNT PUBLISHING

First published by Moon Books, 2022
Moon Books is an imprint of John Hunt Publishing Ltd., No. 3 East Street, Alresford
Hampshire SO24 9EE, UK
office@jhpbooks.net
www.johnhuntpublishing.com
www.moon-books.net

For distributor details and how to order please visit the 'Ordering' section on our website.

Text copyright: Morgan Daimler 2021

ISBN: 978 1 78904 141 5
978 1 78904 142 2 (ebook)
Library of Congress Control Number: 2021935030

A CIP catalogue record for this book is available from the British Library.

Design: Matthew Greenfield

UK: Printed and bound by CPI Group (UK) Ltd, Croydon, CR0 4YY
Printed in North America by CPI GPS partners

We operate a distinctive and ethical publishing philosophy in
all areas of our business, from our global network of authors to
production and worldwide distribution.

Contents

Contents

This book is dedicated to everyone on the Hiddenfolk, Witches, and Elves trip in Iceland.

With thanks to everyone in the Heathen community I am privileged to call a friend.

Author's Note

This book is intended to serve as an introduction to the Norse Gods and to give a reader a basic overview of Heathenry's history, mythology, symbols, and gods as well as its practice in the modern world. In writing this book I have tried to find a balance between academic sources and personal experiences. As someone who has been part of the US Heathen community since 2006, I want my own experiences to inform my writing here so that people can see at least one possible expression of Heathenry in the modern world, but I also want to provide a strong academic resource for readers and a wider view of other possible practices. I have tried to include an extensive bibliography and list a selection of other references that could potentially help readers connect to the Norse Gods in both intellectual and experiential ways and that would be of interest to people curious about Heathenry.

It would be impossible to include everything about either the Norse Gods or Heathenry in a single book of this size, however, I have tried to include what I consider the most pertinent information. Ideally readers will be interested enough to continue researching and reading more, but this book should cover all the essentials. To accomplish this, I am looking at sources spanning both Norse and Germanic cultures, historic and modern, as well as books written by non-academics who feel a strong connection to the subject. I believe that this wide approach is the only way to get a true understanding of Norse Heathenry fully in context.

This book, by nature, will likely tend to reflect my own approach to Heathenry, no matter how I try to avoid bias in my writing, but it should be understood that historic Heathenry was never a homogeneous set of beliefs and practices and that remains true today. There are a multitude of modern Heathen traditions, some of which are at odds with others. I encourage people who are interested to research further into specific approaches.

As with my previous books I am using American Psychological Association (APA) formatting for citations which means that after any quoted or paraphrased material you will see a set of parentheses containing the author's last name and the date the book was published; quoted material will also include the page number the quote was taken from. This can be cross-referenced in the bibliography if you would like to know the source or read it for yourself. I am aware that not everyone likes this style but I prefer it because I find it the most efficient way to reference sources. I am also choosing to use the Anglicized spellings of the deity names throughout although the older culturally specific spellings will be mentioned within the applicable section on each individual deity later in the book. This is because of the wide range of spelling options to be found across the multiple cultures being dealt with in a text on what is effectively pan-Norse mythology.

Introduction

This book is about the Norse pantheon and the systems of belief, historic and modern, that are associated with them. The historic worship of Norse gods was referred to externally as Heathenry;[1] there are many different names for the modern practices including Heathenry, Asatru, and Norse paganism. While there are important nuances between these terms in modern communities, throughout this book the terms heathenry and Norse paganism will be used interchangeably. The term heathen comes from Old English hæðen, meaning 'neither Christian nor Jewish', connected to the Old Norse heiðinn of a similar meaning; while it has been suggested that the term may ultimately mean 'from the heath' it is likely an attempt at glossing the Latin pagan into a Gothic language (Harper, 2021). In effect the term originally meant a rural person or someone uncultured but came to mean a person who wasn't Christian, and in recent years specifically a person who honors the Norse or German gods. It must be noted that the term heathen is used differently in different places. I am using the word here as it is predominantly used in the United States, where heathen and pagan have come to have distinct different meanings in the modern polytheistic communities, however, that does not hold true elsewhere. Readers should make an effort to familiarize themselves with local terms and usages.

In Part I we will be looking at the history, beliefs, and practices of Heathenry and in Part II we will explore who the Norse Gods are as well as related spirits that play an important role in the belief system. These parts are divided fairly equally in this book, as I feel that it is important to both have some basis in the beliefs as well as a solid source for information on the deities and spirits.

Heathenry is a very diverse spirituality and encompasses

everything from people who consider themselves atheists but like the traditions they associate with Heathenry, to people who fully believe in the Norse gods and all the spirits found in Norse mythology and folklore. It also encompasses several distinct cultures including Norse, Anglo-Saxon, and German, all of which will affect the modern practices of the specific groups as well as exactly what deities they believe in and names they use for them. This diversity is a strength but must be clearly understood by anyone seeking to learn about modern Heathenry or about its historic roots, because the various sources and which ones are included or ignored impact the modern forms.

The bulk of this book is centered on the Norse Gods and spirits that are important in Norse belief, as understanding these beings is essential. We will also cover, in less depth, basic cosmology and practice found in Norse paganism to offer a fuller picture of Heathenry. In some places we will touch on things in Anglo-Saxon and German culture as well, particularly where they crossover with, or are important to, wider modern beliefs found in Heathenry. The goal here is not to create an in-depth, one stop resource for the subject but to offer readers a wide range of basic information to give a better understanding of the subject or help beginners seeking a starting place.

Chapter 1

History

Hast thou a friend whom thou trustest well,
from whom thou cravest good?
Share thy mind with him, gifts exchange with him,
fare to find him oft.
- Havamal

The history of Norse paganism and of the Norse pantheon is inextricably linked to the history of the Germanic and Norse peoples themselves. Before we plunge forward into looking at the mythology, cosmology, rituals and practices of Heathenry, and of course the Norse Gods, let's start by looking briefly at the history behind it all. This is by no means intended as a thorough review, only a quick summary, as there is so much material that could be included here.

The term 'Norse' refers to a group of related cultures which share a root language, a branch of the Germanic strand of Indo-European. In previous periods Germanic was the preferred term as it encompasses the entirety of the range of cultures, however, many people conflated Germanic with specifically German and so in recent years I have noted a shift to using Norse as the blanket term instead, although this is less accurate from a semantic perspective. Norse cultures include what in modern terms we would call the countries of Iceland, Norway, Sweden, Finland, Denmark, the Faroe Islands, Shetland Islands, and the Orkney Islands while the broader Germanic would also include Germany, Austria, Switzerland, the Netherlands, Flanders, Frisia, and, historically, cultures which influenced England such as the Anglo-Saxons. These cultures share not only a language root but also other cultural factors including mythological themes, and many of the gods now classified as Norse fit into the broader category of pan-Germanic being found in different iterations across these various cultures.

The language group and cultures originated during the bronze age in the Nordic areas of northern Europe and spread southward over the ensuing centuries. By roughly 500 BCE the languages had become distinct and the cultures were developing in different directions (Harbert, 2006). From there we see the cultural developments becoming more unique between the various forming cultures, which eventually evolved into the material we have today.

When the subject of the Norse cultures is brought up many people immediately equate them to Vikings. This is both accurate and misleading so let's unpack that. The exact meaning of the word Viking is uncertain but by the Middle Ages it was associated with people from Nordic countries who sailed out on raids of other places and was used synonymously with Heathen and Northmen (Hødnebø, 1987). This practice of raiding began around the 8th century CE and went into the 11th century, with England and Ireland being common targets. There are various theories as to why people would become Vikings, including a shortage of available wives and a need for son's outside of the line of inheritance to earn a living or establish themselves, but there's no certainty. It is likely, in my opinion, that several factors were in play and there is no simple explanation to be found.

A Viking was a person who left their home country to sail out and take what could be taken from various other locations, including trade goods, gold, and people (particularly women). This resulted in Norse settlements in several locations including Ireland, the Orkneys, and Iceland, which spread Norse cultural influence further afield. In the case of Ireland, while there were towns and cities founded by the Norse and even a sacred grove dedicated to Thor. Once the Norse were ousted their impact on Irish culture appeared to be limited. In the Orkneys, on the other hand, Norse culture completely overwrote the existing culture and in Iceland created a new and profoundly impactful community. The Viking practice of taking people resulted in an Irish cultural influence[2] in Iceland as so many of the women there had been kidnapped from Ireland or were Irish wives of Norsemen who were part of the Norse settlements in Ireland (Sigurdsson, 2000).

While Vikings tend to get the most attention when Norse culture and paganism is being discussed this is, as was mentioned, slightly misleading. The Vikings were only one facet of the wider cultural milieu and were not a unique culture in themselves but an aspect of shared culture between Norway, Denmark, and Sweden. The impact of the Viking period can't be underrated but we must also be cautious not to romanticize it or extrapolate it out into assumptions about the entirety of Norse cultures and how they operated.

Chapter 2

Mythology

Now the sayings of the High One are uttered in the hall
for the weal of men, for the woe of Jötuns,
Hail, thou who hast spoken! Hail, thou that knowest!
Hail, ye that have hearkened! Use, thou who hast learned!
- Havamal

One of the first things that anyone interested in modern Heathenry will be told by those already practicing it is to study the mythology. While this is not the only route to understanding the Norse gods, it is a vital one because embracing the stories of those gods, even if you don't believe in them, is essential to gaining a fuller picture of who and what they were and are. It is also a good idea to go directly to the source stories for yourself as much as possible rather than depending too much on other people's interpretations or opinions of them, as bias can affect those.

In the broadest strokes Norse mythology tells us about how the worlds were created, various stories of the gods, and the eventual destruction of the Gods in an event called Ragnarök. Norse belief envisions nine worlds, rather than just the one that humans live in, each of which is cosmologically connected on or through a world tree called Yggdrasil; many stories in the Prose and Poetic Eddas feature events across these worlds. Each story is full of detail that teaches us about all of these things as well as about the personalities of the deities, their relationships to each other, and the interconnections between various groups. From a spiritual perspective all of this is vital to have some knowledge of and that's why it's so important, in my opinion, to read at least some of these stories for yourself. Going directly to the source gives you an understanding that can't be gained otherwise.

The Lore

The bulk of modern Norse pagan beliefs are drawn from various sources in mythology, collectively referred to as the lore. How important the lore is depends on the individual or group but in general its fairly heavily weighted by most Heathens, partially because it is as close to any sort of authority across the belief system as you will find. This isn't to say that Heathenry is a fundamentalist religion or a book religion, but rather that the shared mythology is the core that connects people across various specific beliefs and practices.

Prose Edda

One of the most well-known sources that many people look to initially is the Prose Edda, written by Snorri Sturluson in the 13th century. The Prose Edda begins with Snorri Sturluson's pseudohistorical explanation of who the Aesir were, as human beings, and where they came from. This sort of euhemerization is extremely common in Christian material of the time period, which sought to preserve the pagan beliefs of the culture in a way that was acceptable to the church. The best way to do this seemed to be to retell the pagan stories through the lens that the gods were actually very skilled humans.

The opening of the Prose Edda is a section called the Gylfaginning, the deluding of Gylfi, which tells of a mortal man named Gylfi who enters into a discussion with Odin. Through a series of questions and answers Odin relates how reality came to be, how the nine worlds were formed, how all the various beings were created, and various information and stories about the different gods.

The second section is the Skáldskapamal, which contains an assortment of stories, set up as a discourse between Aegir and Bragi. This includes a story of Idunna being kidnapped by

Jotuns and recovered as well as how Skadhi came to be counted among the Aesir.

Poetic Edda

Second to the Prose Edda in popularity is the Poetic Edda, likely having that secondary place because it is slightly more difficult to read than the more straightforward Prose Edda. This text includes a variety of mythic poems, written or collected in Iceland in the 13th century by an unknown author. The material ranges widely but includes the often quoted or popular Havamal, Voluspa, Lokasenna, and Baldrs Draumar [Balder's Dream]. The poems of the Poetic Edda contain a hugely important array of information about the Aesir and related beings.

Saga of the Icelanders

The other major text that falls into the category of lore is the Saga of the Icelanders, a massive collection of stories from Iceland, written between roughly 1200 and 1500 CE. The Sagas cover a wide range of material and stories set in Iceland, many pseudohistorical or historical in nature but often touching on various mythic themes or including the Aesir. For example Odin plays a part in the Saga of King Hrolf Kraki and Egil's Saga references various people going to Valhalla despite not dying as warriors. This is all important information for those seeking to fully understand the range of beliefs.

Some of the most popular individual sagas which touch on Heathen themes or discuss the Norse gods are Egil's Saga, Erik the Red's Saga, Njal's Saga, and the Saga of King Hrolf Kraki.

German Lore

For those with a specifically German focus the main resource tends to be Grimm's Teutonic Mythology, although it was written in the 19th century and is further than the Icelandic material from a pre-Christian time period. Grimm's material should be further checked if possible but overall has proven reasonably accurate within the range of what can be verified. Some also look to Tacitus's Germania as a source, because it was written during the pre-Christian period. However, it is very limited in its scope.

Retellings

Besides the original sources there are also some very good retellings of the myths, particularly the Eddas, to be found. These can be good options for people who find the older sources difficult to get into or understand, but you do want to be sure to find a good retelling that stays as close as possible to the source material. My personal suggestion is Kevin Crossley Hollands book, 'Norse Myths', which recaps the Eddas in a very easy to read way.

Folklore

This chapter is primarily about mythology because mythology is the foundation upon which a lot of Norse paganism is built, however, I would be remiss if I didn't also include or at least touch on folklore as well. Whereas the mythology has survived in only a few forms and in specific recorded versions, the folklore is vast and diverse. Folklore is also extremely regionally specific so we find similarities across the breadth of the stories but also many unique aspects in different areas.

Modern Stories

I also want to add here a quick note about what we may call modern stories. While these are not part of the Lore and often diverge widely from the older beliefs, they can influence what people believe and how they understand the Aesir. A good example of this would be the way that the Marvel movies have influenced and reshaped the way that people understand, particularly, Thor and Loki. While in the mythology the two deities are often depicted travelling together and have a complicated relationship, they are distinctly not brothers, yet I have seen some Heathens believing that they are because of the movies depicting them that way. It's important to understand the powerful influence that popculture and mass media have on spiritual beliefs.

Chapter 3

Cosmology

All will prove true that thou askest of runes –
those that are come from the gods,
which the high Powers wrought, and which Odin painted:
then silence is surely best.
- Havamal

An important aspect to understanding any culture is to look at how that culture understood the world around it within its own context. For our purposes here we are going to look at a variety of key aspects of Norse cosmology which may help the reader better conceptualize the Norse understanding of reality and the world. We will start with the basic idea of sacred space and then move on to more complex ideas relating to the worlds, fate, and the afterlife. Each of these is like a piece of a puzzle which by itself only gives us a small glimpse at the bigger picture they all form together.

Sacred Space

Every religion must have its holy places, affording a means of communication between man, gods, spirits, and forces of nature.
Hilda Ellis Davidson

Sacred space is any place that is set aside for worship, such as a Temple, or a natural place that provides a special connection to Powers beyond ourselves, like a sacred grove. The formation of sacred space may be based in an acknowledgement of a place's inherent sacredness, or may be an entirely human construct where a specific area is declared sacred or made sacred through ritual actions. We find both types of sacred space among the

Norse with references to natural locations like 'Thor's Grove' in Ireland which were seen as holy as well as created spaces like the temple in Uppsala Sweden. The Norse seem to have originally sought out natural sacred spaces for worship and to leave offerings, with the places seen as sacred in this way including clearings in groves of trees, hill tops, and places near bodies of water, swamps, and certain meadows or fields (Ellis Davidson, 1988; Ross, 1970; Ward, 2012.). The Norse continued to favor the use of open sacred spaces for worship until the Christian period, although there are examples of man-made temple structures as well, usually smaller and associated with family use (Ward, 2012.). In Norse cultures we see the creation of fridr-gardr, or peace areas, which were used for worship and also for law courts (Ward, 2012.).

These places were sacred because of an inherent quality recognized by worshipers, such as the presence of specific trees or healing waters, or else were seen as sacred due to omens which occurred to indicate this sacredness or because of specific uses, such as leaving offerings at the sites, which sanctified them. These natural sacred sites might belong to specific Gods or spirits or might be general places of worship (Ward, 2012.).

Constructed sacred spaces might be simple or elaborate. These places were called hofs in the Norse and could be anything from a simple one room wooden building or a large multi-roomed temple (Ward, 2012). Man-made structures were used to honor the Gods with offerings and for community celebrations as well as more natural locations. Although initially they didn't seem to use physical representations of Gods later temple sites included such images, as we see in places like the temple at Uppsala.

The Creation of the Worlds

Norse cosmology, particularly in modern Heathenry, is built off of the mythic cycle as described in the Eddas. This includes a very detailed creation story found in the Gylfaginning and some further details related in the Voluspa which I will try to briefly recap[3] here.

In the beginning there was a great void named Ginnungigap, which was all that existed. Over time to the north of Ginnungigap there came to exist a frozen land called Niflheim and to the south a fiery land called Muspelheim. Heat from Muspelheim drifted into the great void and frozen water from Niflheim flowed in on the other side, so that steam and a heavy frost were created within the gap so that while the north was frozen and inhospitable and the south was burning hot the void became a mild and temperate place. Within this place the melting frost and rain created the first being, a Jotun called Ymir. Ymir fed off of a primordial cow, Audumla, who was also created by the melting frost and ice. And Ymir, being self-generating, began producing offspring thus creating a race of frost Jotuns.

Audumla licked the salty ice for sustenance and as she licked, she revealed another being; after three days Buri was freed from the ice. He was a being different from the Jotuns, described by Snorri as beautiful, great, and mighty. Buri produced a son who in turn married a female Jotun and had three sons: Odin, Vili and Vé. These three killed the primordial Jotun Ymir and used his corpse to create the worlds and the beings within them, so that his blood became the seas, his body and bones the earth and mountains, his skull the bowl of the sky, his brain the clouds, and they set the sun and moon in motion. From the Jotun's corpse came maggots which Odin and his brothers fashioned into the elves and dwarves. Later walking along the new seashore they found two trees washed up, an elm and an ash, and they fashioned these into a human man and woman. And so the worlds and all within them were created.

The World Tree

The world tree is central to Norse cosmology; it is described figuratively as the structure on which the nine worlds exist as well as literally as a tree which is watered and is home to extraordinary animals. The name can be understood as Ygg's horse or steed, with Ygg another name for Odin. Yggdrasil is an ash tree, its roots extend around the worlds of men, Jotuns, and the dead and at its roots rest the well of Urd, from whence the fate of all things come.

It is described this way in the Poetic Edda:

An eagle sits in the limbs of the Ash, and he has understanding of many a thing; and between his eyes sits the hawk that is called Vedrfölnir. The squirrel called Ratatöskr runs up and down the length of the Ash, bearing envious words between the eagle and Nídhöggr; and four harts run in the limbs of the Ash and bite the leaves. They are called thus: Dáinn, Dvalinn, Duneyrr, Durathrór. Moreover, so many serpents are in Hvergelmir with Nídhöggr, that no tongue can tell them, as is here said:

Ash Yggdrasill suffers anguish,
More than men know of:
The stag bites above; on the side it rotteth,
And Nídhöggr gnaws from below.

And it is further said:

More serpents lie under Yggdrasill's stock
Than every unwise ape can think:
Góinn and Móinn (they're Grafvitnir's sons),
Grábakr and Grafvölludr;
Ófnir and Sváfnir I think shall aye
Tear the trunk's twigs.

It is further said that these Norns who dwell by the Well of Urdr take water of the well every day, and with it that clay which lies about the well, and sprinkle it over the Ash, to the end that its limbs shall not wither nor rot; for that water is so holy that all things which come there into the well become as white as the film which lies within the egg-shell

An ash I know, Yggdrasil its name,

With water white is the great tree wet;
Thence come the dews that fall in the dales,
Green by Urth's well does it ever grow. (Brodeur, 1916)

The Nine Worlds

There is some debate about the names of these worlds and what exactly they are but the Prose and Poetic Eddas agree on the number nine. These worlds are most commonly suggested as:

- Midgard – literally 'middle yard', the land of humans.
- Asgard – 'yard of the Aesir', the home of the Aesir, the main gods of Norse mythology. Each of the Aesir has a home in Asgard which is described in varying detail in the mythology. The land is reached by crossing the rainbow bridge of Bifrost which is guarded by the god Heimdall. According to various mythology some mortals do go to Asgard after they die, usually to the hall of a specific deity.[4]
- Vanaheim – 'Vanir's home'- world of the Vanir, a group of deities who were initially at war with the Aesir but later several Vanic deities would join the Aesir. We have little direct information about Vanaheim or the Vanir, excepting the ones who are given to the Aesir as peace-hostages.
- Alfheim or Ljósálfheimr – 'elf home' or 'light elf home', the realm of the Álfar. This world is said to belong to the Vanic god Freyr who received it as a gift.
- Svartálfheim – 'black elf home' land of the dwarves. This realm is also possibly called Niðavellir [new moon fields] again a realm of the dwarves although there is some debate about whether these worlds are synonymous or different places.
- Jotunheim – 'Jotuns home', the land of the Jotuns. Many of the Norse myths take place in Jotunheim either partially

or entirely.

- Muspelheim – land of primordial fire.
- Niflheim – land of primordial ice.
- Helheim – land of the dead. Helheim is ruled by the goddess Hel, a daughter of Loki, who was given charge of it by Odin. All humans who die of age or illness go to Helheim, and while Snorri describes it in deeply unpleasant terms, elsewhere, we see it described as a welcoming place of feasting with the ancestors.

The Grimnismal tells us that Helheim, Jotunheim, and Midgard are at the bottom of the world tree, resting beneath its roots. The array of the other worlds on the tree is less clear.

Ragnarök

A key aspect of Norse cosmology is the idea that the Gods, just like humans, are subject to wyrd and must face inevitable fates. This is expressed through the story of Ragnarök which we find in the Voluspa, or prophecy of the seeress, in the Poetic Edda. In this story Odin goes to speak with a famed seeress who relates to him everything that will happen at the end of the world.

A great, endless winter would fall across the earth as two Jotuns in the form of wolves who chased the sun and moon would catch and devour them. Fenrir, another great Jotun in the form of a wolf and Loki's son, would break the fetters that hold him harmless and two unearthly roosters would crow, one waking the Jotuns to battle and the other rousing the Gods and the heroes in Odin's hall. Loki, who has been bound by the Gods, breaks free and leads the dead from Hel to fight against the Aesir. The fire Jotuns from Muspelheim emerge to fight and their leader, Surt, kills Freyr. Odin is killed by the wolf Fenrir who is in turn killed by Odin's son Vidar, and Thor faces the Midgard serpent Jormungandr; the two kill each other in combat. The sea rises and the earth sinks; Njord returns to the Vanir.

Eventually peace returns to the world and the surviving Gods, notably Thor's children Moði and Magni along with Baldur who has returned from Helheim, begin anew. Humans repopulate and a new sun and moon, children of the ones devoured by the wolves, take to the sky.

In mythology many of Odin's actions are directed at delaying Ragnarök or preparing for it.

Wyrd

It seems that many cultures have some concept relating to a person's purpose or destiny in life, with the culturally specific terms often equated to the English word, fate, which, of course, is the idea of a predestined or predetermined outcome in life which cannot be altered or affected by human action. Many Greek tragedies, such as Oedipus, are based on this idea which is personified in Greek mythology by the Moirae (the Fates) who create the thread of a person's fate, measure it, and cut it at death. In Heathenry the closest idea to fate would be wyrd, but as we shall see it is not exactly the same as the more commonly understood Classical concept.

Wyrd is an Anglo-Saxon word, corresponding to the Norse urd, and means, roughly, *"to come to pass"* or *"becoming"*; related to this is the concept of orlog, meaning *"from the law"*. As it was explained to me, orlog is the sum total of our past actions as well as those of our ancestors - we are born with a fixed orlog based on what has come to pass before our birth. Orlog effects all creation, including the Gods and spirits, as well as people. To quote Bauschatz:

> This past includes the actions of all beings who exist within the enclosing branches of Yggdrasil: men, gods, giants, elves, etc... it is such actions that form the layers or strata that are daily laid in the well by the speaking of the orlog. The coming into the well is orderly and ordered; events are clearly related to each other, and

there is pattern and structure in their storage. (Bauschatz, 1982)

Orlog affects us because it is the base from which we move forward, but wyrd is the active principle created by us during our lives, which in turn creates orlog. Every action we take is based on our wyrd and orlog and further creates the wyrd we are then living with. Wyrd and orlog are both flexible and fixed; like water flowing in a river and the bed of the river itself. The river bed shapes where the river flows and directs the water but the water can change the shape of the river bed. So it is with wyrd; we shape our wyrd by our choices but our wyrd creates orlog which in turn directs our lives. Some people argue that orlog and wyrd are the same concept, and that may be so, I just find that it is easier to grasp them as separate but interlinked concepts. The analogy of weaving is often used to describe wyrd, and I tend to see wyrd as the weft and orlog as the warp. Freewill is an important aspect of wyrd, as we always have choices on how to act within the circumstance we find ourselves in.

Oaths are taken extremely seriously in Heathenry as they are seen as impacting a person's wyrd. To keep an oath strengthens luck and positively impacts the person's wyrd while breaking one weakens their luck. Because of this, if an oath is taken and must be broken the person is usually expected to pay some form of compensation to the person they are breaking the oath to as well, in some cases, to anyone who heard the oath because bearing witness to an oath involves the witness being included in the potential impact of its results. Some Heathens are not comfortable witnessing oaths for this reason and will refuse to be present when they are spoken.

Heathenry and the Afterlife

The afterlife is a very complicated thing in Heathenry, and it is something that is too often simplified in discussions and books to reflect a more classical or monotheistic model. People seem to have an endless desire to know where we go after we die and how we can get there that makes this a perennial question. The answer though is not at all simple because the Heathen understanding of the soul and of the afterlife was not simple.

Many people focus on going to Valhalla, as if Odin's hall was the Heathen equivalent of the Greek Elysian Fields, the reward, the good place that everyone should seek to get to, but that is not so. First of all Odin's hall is described in the Prose Edda as a place of slain warriors, who, for fun, battle each other all day and drink and feast all night (Young, 1964). The mead, literally, flows freely there and the party - and fighting - never ends but it's not a peacefully relaxing place. It is the gathering place of the Einherjar, the warriors who will fight for the Gods during Ragnarök. I tend to imagine it something along the lines of a really rowdy biker bar. It is also only one of many halls and, beyond that, the God's halls themselves are only one possible afterlife destination.

Some people insist that the only way to get to Valhalla is to die in battle, and it is true that the Prose Edda says that the battle dead go there and that Odin sends the Valkyries out to choose those worthy of Valhalla (Young, 1964). However, Freya was said to have her choice of half the battle dead for her hall, Folkvangr as well, meaning that a battle death did not guarantee entrance to Valhalla. And you don't have to die in battle to go to Valhalla as in some cases those who died by other means went there. In Egil's Saga, Egil says that both his sons have gone to Odin's hall, despite the fact that one drowned and one died of a fever; Egil himself, although dedicated to Odin, does not expect to go to Valhalla, but rather says he sees Hel waiting for him (Egil's Saga, 1997). 'Our Troth volume 1' also notes that Sigurdr and Baldr, both killed by weapons, go to Helheim, while Sinfjotli goes to Valhalla after dying of poison (Gundarsson, 2006).

Besides the halls of Odin and Freya several other Gods are specifically mentioned in the Lore. Unmarried maidens might

21

go to Gefjon's hall, as it is said that she is attended by those *"who die maidens"* (Gundarsson, 2006). In the Lay of Harbard, Odin accuses Thor of taking the dead common men into his hall, in contrast to Odin's own preference for warriors, poets, and nobles (Bellows, 2007). Those who drown at sea are taken by Rán, caught up in her nets, and brought to her hall (Grimm, 1966). This gives us a wider picture of where a soul can go after death, but the Gods halls alone are only a small portion of the options available.

The second most well-known destination of the dead is Helheim. The Prose Edda tells us that those who die of old age or illness generally go to Hel's hall, while liars, murderers, and oathbreakers go to Nastrond, both within Helheim (Young, 1964). Odin sent Hel to Niflheim to care for all the dead who came to her, and those who enter her realm belong to her. In the Edda Helheim is described as gloomy and terrible, yet elsewhere in other stories, such as Baldr's Dream, it is described as a rich feasting hall, with ale ready to welcome guests (Bellows, 2007; Young, 1964). I tend to believe the warm, welcoming version of Hel's hall is far more likely and I see Helheim as the realm of the ancestors.

Some dead become mound dwellers; their souls going into the land. In Eyrbyggja Saga after Thorolfr's son drowns it is believed he goes into a hill on his father's land where he is welcomed with feasting (Eyrbyggja Saga, 1972). In Gisli Saga, a man who is called a friend of Freyr dies and is buried in a mound and it is said that no frost will form on the hill because Freyr does not want frost to come between them (Our Troth, 2006). In the Voluspa, Odin goes to get the prophecy from an ancient seer in a mound and, indeed, the entire process of utiseta is based on the idea of contacting spirits within grave mounds. Additionally it has been suggested that some Álfar are the male dead of a family as the Dísir are the female dead (Gundarsson, 2006). Speaking of Dísir, it is entirely possible for a woman, after death, to become a dísir, or dís, that is a specific type of spirit that watches over her family line (Gundarsson, 2006).

Reincarnation is also an old Heathen belief. Specifically it is believed that a soul might be reborn within a family line and that naming a child after a deceased ancestor can mean the rebirth of that ancestor in the child (Ellis Davidson, 1968). In some cases a child might be born with similar marks or the appearance of a deceased family member which could indicate a soul relationship (Gundarsson, 2006). I have also heard it said that it was considered bad luck to name a child after a living relative for this reason.

It is clear that there are a wide array of possible places for a soul to go after death. As individuals we do not seem to have much real control over where we might go when we die, so I honestly don't see the point in worrying much about it. Live a good honorable life while you are here and worry about the afterlife when you get there.

Chapter 4

Ritual

Better ask for too little than offer too much,
like the gift should be the boon;
better not to send than to overspend.
- Havamal

Heathen rituals have no set format but there are broad strokes that seem to have been used historically and which modern groups have adopted. This chapter will look at those, but readers should understand that none of this is written in stone. Specific traditions or groups will have their own particular approaches.

The core idea behind heathen rituals is reciprocity, the concept that things should be in balance and that therefore a gift requires a gift in return. The gods give to us and we give back to them. All ritual, at its heart, should serve the dual purposes of honoring the Gods and of opening us to Their blessing. It should also allow us to be aware of and reflect on our connection to those Powers and our part in the natural and cosmic cycles.

Heathens may practice alone or in groups. What a group is called will vary but the most common term I have seen is Kindred, and its structure will be based on the tradition the people in it belong to as well as the preferences of the people in it. Some kindreds are very hierarchical, being led by a gothi or gythia [priest or priestess] while others may be more egalitarian. The style of group and number of members will have some influence over how rituals are done. I should also note here that some kindreds and traditions have a very set idea of what beings can or cannot be invoked or acknowledged in a ritual, with Loki often being a controversial figure[5].

Ritual Equipment

As with all spiritual traditions there are a few specialized or specially named tools that can be found in Heathen ritual. None of these are essential but they are commonly used so helpful to be aware of. And of course you can use any or all of them if you choose to.

- Altar – called a vé, many rituals will centre on some form of an altar. This may be as simple as a flat surface that holds the ritual tools being used to something much more elaborate featuring whatever decorations a person or group prefers.
- Horn – a drinking horn is the standard method of making offerings, which is usually something like mead.[6]
- Ritual Bowl – a bowl used to collect the liquid offerings as they are made.
- Hammer – a symbolic representation of Thor's Hammer used for blessing, consecrating, and protecting spaces.
- Oath ring – A special armband sized ring on which oaths are made.

Rituals

Blót & Faining

A blót is the most common form of ritual found across Heathenry, and centres on a sacrificial ritual; historically that sacrifice would have been of a farm animal but in modern Heathenry it is more often an offering of something else, usually mead. For some Heathens a true blót must involve animal sacrifice and anything else would be called a faining. A blót or faining may be held to the Gods, Álfar, land spirits, or ancestors, as well as any other type of spirit acknowledged in the belief system that is thought to be able to help humans or who humans may need to propitiate. For example, we have historic evidence of ritual sacrifices to the Gods and Álfar for positive or helpful things but we also have accounts in Iceland of sacrifices being made to dangerous powers, such as those associated with volcanos, asking that they remain harmless.

We do have some basic information about how blóts would have been conducted historically. For example, this description from one of the sagas:

> It was an old custom, that when there was to be sacrifice all the bóndis [freeholders] should come to the spot where the temple stood and bring with them all that they required while the festival of the sacrifice lasted. To this festival all the men brought ale with them; and all kinds of cattle, as well as horses, were slaughtered, and all the blood that came from them was called hlaut, and the vessels in which it was collected were called hlaut-vessels. Hlaut-staves were made, like sprinkling brushes, with which the whole of the altars and the temple walls, both outside and inside, were sprinkled over, and also the people were sprinkled with the blood; but the flesh was boiled into savoury meat for those present. The fire was in the middle of the floor of the temple, and over it hung the kettles, and the full goblets were handed across the fire; and he who made the feast, and was a chief, blessed the full goblets, and all the meat of the sacrifice.

Hákon the Good's Saga, section 16, Sacred Texts website.

In general a blót or faining will follow something close to this outline:

1. Blessing or hallowing the space. The first step is to bless or hallow the space, which can be done in various ways. Some groups use something called the Hammer Rite, a 20th century practice that involved facing each direction, tracing the shape of Thor's Hammer in the air, and calling on Thor to protect and bless the space[7]. Some others may asperge the space or burn herbs associated with cleansing

and blessing. Others may simply use a prayer or chant to call on various powers to bless or consecrate the space.

2. Invoke the deities or powers being offered to. Next the person leading the ritual will invoke the deities being honoured on that occasion. Some groups choose to limit the invoked beings to only the ones directly being offered to while other may also include land spirits and ancestors as well. As each one is invoked a bit of mead may be poured out for them.

3. Pass horn and make offerings. The horn is passed to the members of the group who each raise the horn and say something fitting to the occasion. After speaking they either drink from the horn, or if they prefer not to drink, they may kiss the rim of the horn.

4. Pour offerings out to the gods. When the ritual is finished the mead that has been poured into the offering bowl is taken and poured out onto the earth. I was taught that when doing this we say *"From the Gods to the earth to us, from us to the earth to the Gods. A gift for a gift."* This is only a basic outline and while the structure is generally close to this, at least in my experience, the details may vary. For example a ritual fire may be used instead of an offering bowl, with offerings being (carefully) placed in the flames. I have attended rituals that use that approach, with people offering written prayers, poems, and physical items to the fire instead of pouring out mead.

A Simple Faining

My kindred tends to use a basic structure, which I will describe here. After blessing the space we always start by hailing the ancestors, land spirits, and Gods, pouring out offerings from the horn to each as they are named. We go around after they are hailed and we each say what we want or need to about why we are gathered, drink from the horn or kiss it, and may make additional offerings. When we have all said as much as we feel we need to we take the collected offerings out and pour them onto our outdoor altar space while thanking the gods and spirits for their blessings. Then we feast, usually a pot-luck style meal together (some of this food is also offered later).

Sumbel

The other main ritual form found in Heathenry is the sumbel. A modern sumbel follows a basic format wherein a horn of mead (or other beverage) is passed around the group at least three times; each time as the horn comes to a person, they say something then drink from the horn. The first time each person praises either a specific deity or the deity of their choice, depending on the wider approach of the sumbel. The second round each person praises their ancestors either in general or one specifically by name. The third round, and any subsequent rounds, is for boasting.

This is a description of a basic sumbel from one of the sagas:

> And first Odin's goblet was emptied for victory and power to his king; thereafter, Niord's and Freyja's goblets for peace and a good season. Then it was the custom of many to empty the brage-goblet; and then the guests emptied a goblet to the memory of departed friends, called the remembrance goblet. Hákon the Good's Saga, section 16, Sacred Texts website

Some people combine a blót and sumbel or a faining and sumbel or otherwise merge the types of rituals, while others are adamant in keeping them separate.

Offerings

Why do we make offerings? The main reason historically was twofold: to propitiate the spirits for blessing or to prevent harm, or to maintain an agreed upon exchange. In the first case, when applied to the Norse gods, the idea was that if we offered to them willingly, they would be obligated by reciprocity to return that gift with another. This is of course a very simplified explanation, but it is something we see playing out in mythology. For example, in the Lay of Hyndla, Freya admits that she is going to such lengths to answer the prayer of her follower, Ottar, because he has offered so much to her that the liquid flowing across her stone altar has made the structure look like it's made of glass. The second aspect of this is more esoteric but is built on the concept of an historic exchange between humans and Gods which creates an obligation. In this case it is less that the Gods will directly punish a person for failing to keep up the obligation as that changing allegiance changes a person's fate. We see this in the idea that some Heathens refused to convert to Christianity because they believed it would cut them off from their ancestors and deny then a reunion with their deceased family after death. These concepts are also layered into the idea that to deny the gods an expected offering or include an outsider in worship may offend them possibly as a breach of an obligation, such as we see in the account of the Alfablót where the traveller seeking shelter was turned away, despite the deep-seated expectations of hospitality, because he was a Christian and the household was celebrating the Alfablót and feared offending the Gods.

With the Gods we may be offering for many reasons but ultimately the ideas can be the same: to build relationships, to create connection, in thanks, in propitiation. Offerings to other types of spirits are motived for various reasons but often as part of a request of some sort. Offering to the ancestors may be more casual and more often because the relationship with them is closer and more implicit. Reciprocity is built piece by piece in giving when things are received and offerings are important to that.

In a Heathen context, offerings can be broken down into two main types, those done by groups and those done by individuals. Group offerings are usually done in a ritual setting as part of a blót. Individual offerings may be done at any time

Any offering should always be the best of something that you have to give, even if it's a minor offering you are making. The idea here isn't to do something as a throw away action but to do it with intention and even if its small and casual it should be meaningful. It should have value, both intrinsically and to you as something that actually costs to give. The cost doesn't have to be monetary but it should be something that really matters to you, something that you have an investment in. For example if you were offering mead (a common choice) you would want to give the best quality you could find or make. I have personally also offered poetry and art in the past and when doing so I make sure to burn the only copy so that it is a real sacrifice. Offering to spirits is not a matter of giving second rate things or whatever you have on hand[8], although I will say that in some situations, I have literally given the jewelry I was wearing. In my house we often share our own food with the various spirits we offer to, both in the belief that we are giving what is good enough for us, and because the practice of sharing food with spirits is a long one in many cultures and may be seen in ancient ritual sites were evidence shows feasting and faunal deposits (people sacrificing animals, eating them and giving them to the gods).

Chapter 5

Celebrations & Prayers

Most dear is fire to the sons of men,
most sweet the sight of the sun;
good is health if one can but keep it,
and to live a life without shame.
- Havamal

Modern Norse Heathenry is a diverse thing and encompasses a wide range of beliefs and practices that may share nothing in common except the Gods that are acknowledged and the core practices followed. There is no universally agreed on set of holy days, ritual practices, or prayers, and often the specific type of Heathenry or region of practice will shape how these things are approached. What I am going to include here is a very general overview of both a Norse approach and a German approach to holidays, as examples, as well as some discussion of rituals for major life events, and examples of prayers.

Holy Days

There is no official or agreed upon calendar of Heathen holidays although there is a rough consensus. It must be kept in mind though that we don't have enough concrete information on the historic practices to know with certainty what the cycle of holy days then was and all of the modern calendars of celebrations are reconstructions that are heavily influenced by the person creating them. Specific traditions and particular cultural approaches will have their own ideas about holy days. Many of these calendars blend folklore and references from multiple Nordic cultures as well as modern interpretations of themes and beings in ways that mean even two groups celebrating the same holy day may have very different understandings of why and how.

We have a handful of references to historic Heathen holy days, coming to us largely from the Ynglinga Saga, and the exact timing of these is difficult to sort out beyond the seasons they occurred in:

> There should be a sacrifice at the beginning of winter for a good year, and in the middle of winter for a good crop, the third in summer day, that was the sacrifice for victory.

There are also textual references to Alfablót and Dísirblót, although again the exact timing of each is not specified.

There are several other holidays that have often been added to that list based on later folk traditions and these can include: Yule (which may or may not be the midwinter celebration referenced above), Ostara, Winter Finding, and Winter Nights. Additionally some Heathens choose to celebrate particular days in honour of historic figures or events, for example, 9 April in memory of Hákon Sigurðurdsson who was seen as a great defender of Heathenry (Gundarsson, 2007).

Below I will give a short overview of some of the more popular or common modern Heathen holidays:

Yule

In Germanic and Norse traditions Yule is a 13-night, 12-day festival that is considered one of the most sacred times of the year. For most heathens[9] Yule begins on Mother Night, the night before the solstice which is often celebrated in honor of Frigga and the Dísir. Many modern heathens that I know choose to stay up on the night before the solstice in order to greet the dawn on the solstice morning. The day of the solstice itself is considered both the most powerful of Yule and also the most dangerous as both trolls and ghosts are roaming free on the night of Yule. On this day the Yule log is burnt and the most sacred oaths are sworn. Celebrations continue until New Year's, a day that itself is important since it sets the tone for the year to come; actions taken on the last day of Yule/New Year's eve (or day) influence the year to come.

Swearing oaths and making sacred toasts were sacred activities, as well as leaving out food offerings for the gods and spirits. Odin was especially associated with Yule time, as are the goddesses Perchte, Berchte or Holda. Yule bucks were made (the mask of a goat head, or a straw goat) and used for guising but was also believed to have its own separate spirit that had to be propitiated - often with ale or porridge - in order not to harm anyone in the family. Porridge is also left out as an offering to the house wight or spirit that lives in the home. A Yule tree was used for decoration and a yule log was burnt or in some modern cases a log is set with candles which are burnt.

Disablót

A celebration dedicated to the Dísir, protective female spirits. Many Heathens choose to place this celebration in February, in line with the Swedish celebration of Disting which is thought to be rooted in the older Heathen celebration of the Dísir. Others, however, may time it with either of the equinoxes. References to a holiday for the Dísir can be found in several sources, although the sources do not make the timing of the holiday clear, leaving it up to the individual or group to choose when to celebrate.

Although modern Dísirblóts tend to be more family and personally focused, the historic evidence supports large community events that would have included fairs and public celebration, such as Snorri describes in the Heimskringla and which we see described in the Ynglinga Saga. The Dísir were important spirits which guard over a person and their family's luck and can influence success or give warnings of danger.

Ostara

Based on the writings of Grimm in his Teutonic Mythology books, Ostara is a holiday that has been largely reconstructed from later (19th century) German folk practices and Grimm's speculation about a goddess of the same name as well as a mention of a similarly named Eostre among the Anglo-Saxons. Bede has this to say about Eostre and her holy day:

> *Eosturmonath has a name which is now translated "Paschal month", and which was once called after a goddess of theirs named Eostre, in whose honour feasts were celebrated in that month. Now they designate that Paschal season by her name, calling the joys of the new rite by the time-honoured name of the old observance.* (Wallis, 1999)

Because little is known about the original holiday or the goddess people who celebrate today tend to look at more recent folk practices for inspiration and the wider themes around the return of spring.

Walburgisnacht

A German pagan holiday, although it has been more widely embraced. In Teutonic Mythology, Grimm discusses at length the way that these two halves, personified as *"Herr Summer"* and *"Herr Winter"* battle against each other with each one winning dominance over half the year (Grimm, 1888). Grimm emphasizes May Day as the beginning of summer,

> *Again, as summer begins with May, we have that month acting as its representative, and just as full of life and personality."* (Grimm, 1888). And also discusses its importance as a holiday, *"Everything goes to prove, that the approach of summer was to our forefathers a holy tide, welcomed by sacrifices, feast and dance, and largely governing and brightening the people's life.* (Grimm, 1888)

In modern parlance the German pagan holiday is usually called Walburgisnacht or Walpurgisnacht. This name is certainly related to a saint and her saint's day[10] and possibly to an older pagan Goddess. The holiday is usually dated beginning on April 30th and going into May 1st, and this date is the one most widely used. In Teutonic Mythology, however, we see that the celebration was based on the blooming of certain flowers or the return of certain birds. This may show that originally the celebration's timing was based on environmental signs that would have varied by region, explaining why Grimm mentions May 1st but also gives no specific date and talks about some of the associated traditions being seen as early as March in southern areas. As Grimm says:

> But the coming in of Summer did not happen on any fixed day of the year, it was determined by accidental signs, the opening of flowers, the arrival of birds. This was called finding Summer: 'ich hân den Sumer vunden,' (Grimm, 1888).

The focus of May Day is on welcoming back summer and celebrating the return of warm weather and its life affirming qualities. At this time some believe that the Wild Hunt leaves until the next winter, leaving behind a single hound called the Windhund who brings good weather, fertility and luck (Hodge, n.d.) This hound may be associated with several different goddesses including Frau Gode, Berchta, and Frikke and is offered a slice of bread with butter and honey on May Day to ensure its blessing on the home (Hodge, n.d). The night of April 30th is particularly associated with witches, who were said to gather to celebrate and in a modern context is considered a time of magic and enchantment. These witches were seen as honoring or belonging to Holda (Grimm, 1888). Any or all of these goddesses might be honored by modern Germanic Heathens.

There are many traditions associated with this holiday, too many for me to discuss here. We can, however, break the traditions down into roughly two types: those that banish winter and welcome summer, and those designed to bless or protect the new season. Some of the first type are mentioned by Grimm and include wagon processions welcoming summer, the ritual drowning of winter personified as *"death"*, a mock fight between two people dressed as Winter and Summer where summer prevails, and the singing of songs (Grimm, 1888). These songs may be short chants, such as *"'Sommer' rein, Winter' naus!'"* - summer come in, winter go out! - or may be longer (Grimm, 1888). The second type of tradition includes offerings to the spirit hound left by the Wild Hunt, burning old worn-out tools, blessing bonfires which may be jumped over, the creation of May bushes - that is a small bush or decorated branch covered in yellow ribbons, flowers, and eggshells - and the gathering of flowers brought in to bless the house (Grimm, 1888; Hodge, n.d.)

There is a possibility that, like Yule, Walburgisnacht was originally a 12-day holiday. This would be in keeping with the amount of material that Grimm includes in his section on Summer, traditions which would be hard, if not impossible, to celebrate in a single day. Grimm also specifically mentions, in his section on witches:

The Witches' Excursion takes place on the first night in May... They ride up Blocksberg on the first of May, and in 12 days must dance the snow away; then Spring begins. (Grimm, 1888).

This may indicate a belief that the welcoming of summer was a process of banishing winter, and only after rituals being done over the right amount of time - 12 days - would winter actually retreat and summer begin. In the German-American practice of Urglaawe the holiday includes the 12 nights of Wonnetdanz where certain frost Jotuns fight against the thawing of the land and are repelled each night (Schreiwer, 2013). Looking at the wider scope of German practices from March to May, they begin with the holiday of Ostara and end with Walburgisnacht.

Midsummer

A celebration of the longest day and shortest night which occurs on the summer solstice. The date for this varies slightly every year but occurs between 20 June and 23 June; there has also been speculation that popular saints' days that fall very close to these days, such as Saint John's Day on 24 June, also incorporate displaced summer solstice traditions. This would fit a wider pattern of people preserving their folk traditions by shifting them to a veneer of acceptable Christianity.

Much of the information we have on potentially pre-Christian Heathen rites on Midsummer come from Christian writers criticizing or denouncing such celebrations. The 7th century text Vita Eligii encourages Christians not to participate in Heathen bonfires or the dancing and singing that occurred at them, for example (Gundarsson, 2007). Bonfires are a widespread custom of midsummer, found not only across Germanic and Norse areas but across Celtic language speaking ones as well. Bonfire traditions may include jumping over the flames for luck and fertility as well as to symbolize the power of the sun or deities connected to it.

In some folklore midsummer was connected to the Wild Hunt being more active and travelling abroad, lending an air of danger to the shortest night.

Álfablót

There is a long and reasonably well documented history of offering to the elves which can be described as a more formal religious ritual or sacrifice. In the 11th century Austrfararvísur, there is a passage which recounts the story of a Christian traveler who is turned away from a Swedish home because the family is celebrating an álfablót and fears to offend the Gods by allowing the unbeliever in (Hall, 2007). This may be the sacrifice mentioned in Ynglinga Saga, which occurred at the end of autumn for a good year. Evidence suggests that the Swedish álfablót took place in late autumn; additionally there is a reference in Kormak's Saga involving an injured man who was offering a bull sacrifice to the elves in hope of healing.

> *It appears even that to these black elves in particular, i.e., mountain spirits, who in various ways came into contact with man, a distinct reverence was paid, a species of worship, traces of which lasted down to recent times. The clearest evidence of this is found in the Kormakssaga p. 216-8. The hill of the elves, like the altar of a god, is to be reddened with the blood of a slaughtered bull, and of the animal's flesh a feast prepared for the elves.... An actual âlfabôt. With this I connect the superstitious custom of cooking food for angels, and setting it for them. So there is a table covered and a pot of food placed for home-smiths and kobolds; meat and drink for domina Abundia; money or bread deposited in the caves of subterraneans, in going past.* Grimm, Teutonic Mythology

Evidence suggests that the Swedish álfarblót took place in late autumn; additionally in the quote mentioned above by Grimm the reference from Kormak's Saga involved an injured man who was offering a bull sacrifice to the elves in hope of healing (Gundarsson, 2007). There is also an account from Norway from 1909 of a man whose family sacrificed a cow to 'the mound dwellers' when his father died (Gundarsson, 2007). This indicates that álfablóts were possibly both seasonal and done when need dictated.

In many modern Heathen groups álfablóts are used to honour the male ancestors in a way similar to the female ancestors, although its speculative that the Álfar are male ancestral dead rather than non-human beings.

Winter Finding

Possibly the modern version of Haust blót, *"autumn sacrifice"*, mentioned in the Ynglinga saga and in other texts, Winter Finding is usually celebrated on the autumn equinox and is a harvest celebration. In the countries where this holiday is originally found late September into early October would have been the beginning of winter, making the name of the holy day apt. It would centre on honouring the abundance of the harvest and the crops that had been brought in.

Winter Nights

Also possibly the modern version of Haust Blót, as the timing is uncertain, Winter Nights represents the end of the harvest and would likely have originally occurred around the middle of October. In modern practice it may be used as a time to connect to ancestors and has been compared to the Celtic festival of Samhain (Gundarsson, 2007). Many of the traditions associated with it are similar to ones found in wider folk practices celebrating or connecting to the ancestors.

Pregnancy and Birth

There is not a lot of information to be found on traditional pregnancy practices in the Norse. One possible explanation for this that, like many cultures of the time period, a child was not seen as person until they had survived a certain amount of time after birth and been recognized or acknowledged by the family, particularly the father (Gundarsson, 2007). This is logical given the high rates of infant mortality, and also allowed for the newborn to be killed or exposed if it was unwanted, sickly, or unacceptable to the parents (after a child was officially acknowledged such actions would be treated as murder). Although extremely harsh and unacceptable to modern heathens such infanticide of newborns was a widespread practice in most, if not all, ancient cultures. The result of this for a modern Heathen seeking traditional pregnancy practices may be that there just isn't that much to be found, although there is more in the category of birth practices and child blessings.

One practice that can be found in Sweden was done by a woman in her 7th month of pregnancy. The mother-to-be would draw blood from her finger with a needle and use the blood to draw protective runes on a piece of wood, before spinning three lengths of linen thread (Ward, 2012). One length of thread would be left white, another dyed red, and the third dyed black, while the rune blooded wood would be burned and the ashes added to beer or mead (Ward, 2012). The sections of linen thread were burned apart into 7 inch threads using a brand from the fire, soaked in boiling salt water, and then left to dry in the branches of a tree for 3 days (Ward, 2012). The threads were carefully saved until the day of the birth when the black threads, representing death and bad luck, were burned and the ashes buried, the white thread was used to tie the cord at birth, and the red was strung with a bead [probably amber] and tied on the baby's wrist for protection (Ward, 2012). This one would actually work just as well in a modern context, although I suppose for those of us that don't spin, we would have to buy the needed thread/yarn.

When it comes to birth there are several practices for modern people that are based on older folklore and mythology. The Troth, for example, suggests making a prayer and offering to Frigga and the Dísir at the onset of labor (Gundarsson, 2007). Silver keys are cited as a common charm for childbirth, using the symbolism of unlocking the birth passage and encouraging a speedy and easy birth (Gundarsson, 2007). A common plant used to make the bed for childbirth is called *"Freyar gras"* (Freya's Weed) associating Freya with childbirth as well, so that a laboring woman might call on Frigga, Freya, and the Dísir for support and aid (Gundarsson, 2007). There is a strong folk tradition in both Germany and Scotland that all doors should be unlocked, as a locked door could block the birth process (Gundarsson, 2007). The mother might also choose to wear keys, perhaps as jewelry, during labor and should also be sure to untie and unknot everything that she can in her room as knots are also thought to delay or complicate the birth. Even the hair might be kept loose to avoid any possible ties or knots.

There are also runes associated with childbirth. In Sigdrifumal it says:

You shall know birth runes, if you would give help in birthing, and loosen a child from the woman. You shall rest them on the palm, and on the hand's span, and bid the dísir's aid.

Of course the actual birth runes being referred to are unknown now but different modern authors have suggested possibilities. Perthro and Berkano are often mentioned as birth runes, and it is possible to make a birth bindrune using Perthro, Berkano, and Laguz, with Perthro opening downward to indicate an open passage for the child (Gundarsson, 2007). Naudhiz is also mentioned as a birth rune, being associated with need and with the Norns; I have heard it suggested to draw Naudhiz on the hands or even paint it on the fingernails to aid in birth. Otherwise the runes chosen can be drawn or traced on the hands of those helping and on the abdomen of the laboring woman.

Other types of birth magic include galdoring the birth runes during labor, as well as writing prayers or birth spells on paper or parchment and placing it with the mother (Gundarsson, 2007). The prayers could be written ahead of time by the mother and could include re-paganized versions of older birth prayers. For example, this prayer, though Christian, could be adapted: *"Virgin Mary, gentle mother, loan your keys to me; to open my limbs and my members."* (Ellis Davidson, 1998).

This could perhaps be re-written as *"Frigga, mighty Lady, loan me your keys: to open my limbs and ease this birth."*

There are different folktales, such as Sleeping Beauty, that reflect the older heathen ideas about the way that the Norns could affect the fate of a newborn. In modern practice perhaps a person would want to hold a blót or similar type ritual to the Norns after the birth to ask for blessings and good wyrd for the baby. It might also be worth considering setting up a small altar to the Norns during pregnancy for a similar purpose. It would be traditional to keep the placenta and bury it near a tree (Ward, 2012). For a modern heathen this could perhaps be done instead by planting a new tree over the placenta. Additionally a modern heathen might choose to adapt the American custom of the baby shower by setting up a small altar to the Norns and asking each guest to offer a blessing for the baby, perhaps written on a piece of paper that could be placed on the altar. This sort of petitioning the Norns for good wyrd for the baby would reflect the older idea of the Norns as weaving the new child's wyrd.

Marriage

There is no directly preserved account of an entire historic Heathen wedding ceremony but we do have some general ideas of what probably was involved. Marriage during the Viking period was a matter of agreements and alliances between families, where love, or even liking between the couple, was not required[11] (Ward, 2021). Hopefully this is no longer true but it does affect the way we must understand the historic evidence we have.

The bulk of the written material that has been preserved deals not with marriage but with courtship and marriage negotiation (Ward, 2021). This means that for modern couples seeking to have a Heathen wedding the best sources to look to are hints in the mythology. It also means that much must be approached creatively.

The general format for a wedding would involve not only the exchange of vows but of the gift of a sword to the bride from the groom, to be held for her future child and the drinking of mead (Ward, 2021). The wedding represented the leaving behind of the couple's previous life and allegiances and the formation of new loyalties and a new phase of life. The oaths the couple would take were, of course, taken very seriously and expected to be adhered to[12], something that modern couples should also consider when deciding what vows to use. If we follow suggestions from mythology then Thor's Hammer would be used to bless the bride either in the ceremony or during the reception/feast that follows.

Ward in the article 'Courtship, Love, and Marriage in Viking Scandinavia' outlines a thoroughly reconstructed wedding ceremony. The book, 'Our Troth volume 2', also offers ideas for modern Heathen wedding formats.

Funerals

There are no set prescribed funeral practices or beliefs in Heathenry so when a person dies it is their personal preferences or the traditions within their group that would need to be considered. As with marriage practices, we don't have preserved accounts of full ceremonies of this nature, although we do have archeology that can give us some ideas of the general concepts around the subject.

From a historic perspective we see that the two main funeral forms seem to have been ceremonial cremation on a pyre or boat[13] or burial with grave goods. Modern Heathens may choose to be cremated following local laws or may choose burial in which case they could request that personal items be buried with them in the style of grave goods. I have seen this done on occasion.

This passage from the Havamal is a popular one with many modern Heathens both for funerals and as a prayer for those who have passed:

Cattle die and kinsmen die,
thyself too soon must die,
but one thing never, I ween, will die, –
fair fame of one who has earned.

Cattle die and kinsmen die,
thyself too soon must die,
but one thing never, I ween, will die, –
the doom on each one dead.

Prayers

Prayer can feature as a significant aspect of Heathenry for some people, as they seek to connect to the deities of the Norse pantheon. Others may find prayer superfluous and many fall somewhere in between essential and unimportant. We do have accounts of Heathens praying and we know that they built temples and used statues to represent their deities, which were sometimes prayed to. For example one man, Thórólfr, approaching Iceland, prayed for guidance on where to land then threw his god-pillars overboard and followed where they led him. We also have examples from the conversion period of people praying to Thor against Christian priests. In this section we will look at a few examples of historic material used for prayer and also of some modern prayers.

Historic Prayers
We don't have many examples of historic prayers or charms that explicitly call on the Norse gods but we do have some. I am going to include a sample of them here for people to see and also use.

Sigdrifa's Prayer
Hail Day!
Hail sons of Day!
Hail Night and her daughters!
Look on us here
With loving eyes.
Grant to us victory.
Hail to the Gods!
Hail to the Goddesses

And all the generous Earth!
Give to us wisdom
and goodly speech,
And healing hands, all our lives.

Healing prayer: The second Merseburg Charm

Phol and Wodan were riding to the woods,
and the foot of Balder's foal was sprained
So Sinthgunt, Sunna's sister, conjured it.
and Frija, Volla's sister, conjured it.
and Wodan conjured it, as well he could:
Like bone-sprain, so blood-sprain,
so joint-sprain:
Bone to bone, blood to blood,
joints to joints, so may they be glued. (Fortson, 2004)

Modern Prayers

There are also many modern prayers that people might use and, of course, you may always make up your own. In the following section I am including a selection of prayers I have written as examples.

Prayer to Eir for Healing

Eir, greatest of healers,
Let me be healthy and hale
Let me be well and whole
Let me be fine and fit
May illness leave me
May wellness find me

Prayer to Eir for a Chronically Ill Child

Gentle goddess of healing
Be with my child (name)
I offer you this (name offering)

45

That you will help her
Give her strength
Give her hardiness
Give her vitality
As she fights for health
Gentle goddess of healing
Eir, be with my child

Prayer to Eir for Herbal Medicine

Eir, goddess of the mortar and pestle
As a mix this medicine,
as I blend these herbs,
May they be blessed
May they bring healing
May they bring health
In your name, Eir
May it be so

Prayer to Odin for Writing

Grant me,
winner of Odrerir,
the poet's power
Let words be my weapons,
sharp, strong, and well-aimed,
May my meaning be clear
May my message be persuasive,
May my methods be enchanting,
Odin, grant me inspiration

Prayer for Travel

Wodan, wandering God
May my way be clear before me
Donar, God of might and main
May your hammer ward my way

Zui, great God and guiding star,
May I travel timely along my way
Safely I go forth,
Safely I shall return
By my will, it is so

Prayer for Wisdom

Harbard, Wise Ferryman,
Help me learn patience
Help me learn to answer well
Help me find my wisdom
Greybeard, May it be so

Prayer for Abundance

Oski, Wish-giver, Will-worker,
I seek security and safety
I want my income to be sound
I am open to your guidance and gifts
May I find the blessings I seek
May my hard work be worthwhile
May my effort be rewarded
With abundance and prosperity

Invocation to Wodan[14]

Wodan, Wanderer, Wise one,
I call to you
Hanged one, Hidden one, High one,
I call to you
Yule father, All father, Victory father
I call to you
Mighty God, I invoke you
Ancient One, I offer to you
Wand-bearer, I honor you

Chapter 6

Norse Magic

Dost know how to write, dost know how to read,
dost know how to paint, dost know how to prove,
dost know how to ask, dost know how to offer,
dost know how to send, dost know how to spend?
- Havamal

Magic in a Norse context is a complex subject and one that can be controversial. There are those in Heathenry that feel magical practice has no place and those who find it central. For our purposes here we will be looking at five types of magic that are attested to historically, how they were used and how they may be used in modern times.

Seidhr

Seidhr is a practice that existed historically and that has been reconstructed in modern heathenry, although how close or distant the historic practice is from the modern version is debatable. Most of the mythic and folkloric references are vague or require interpretation, leaving reconstruction open to adaptation and variations. Modern seidhr has become a rather unique practice in itself, separate from the historic model, and often including practices that have been innovated by the people attempting to recreate the older concept. It is also worth noting that the practice of modern seidhr is often controversial, in part because the historic practice was also viewed as controversial and on the boundaries of society.

Defining the word is complicated because there is no straightforward etymology and people usually resort to comparing it to other cultural practices like shamanism[15]. In truth seidhr is its own type of magical practice and isn't really comparable to other cultural forms, which all either include things seidhr doesn't do or exclude things seidhr does do. Cat Heath in the book 'Elves, Witches & Gods' defines seidhr this way:

[a] *word for magic, or more specifically a magic of binding or pulling that was connected to spinning in some contexts."* (Heath, 2021, p 321)

I have found this to be the most accurate description of the practice.

According to the references we have in the Lore, seidhr might include weather working, talking to spirits, and manipulation of people's minds in various ways, from altering their perceptions to influencing their actions. For example, in one account a woman confuses the sense of men hunting her son by making him look like a staff or rod leaning against a wall so that they leave without harming him (at least initially).

Oracular work was closely related to this, although it sometimes fell under the different name of spae or spá[16]. The best extant account of this style oracular work is found in Erik the Red's Saga, where we see a woman travelling around to various homesteads and, if treated properly, preforming as an oracle for them to tell of the coming year. The process for this was complicated and involved, among other things, the seeress eating the hearts of one of each of the animals on the farm, specific songs being sung to call the spirits, and the seeress then relaying messages from them. There have been several modern efforts to recreate this style of oracular work with diverse approaches to the method.

Runes

"Songs and runes then can do very great things. They are able to kill and bring to life, as well as prevent from dying; to heal or make

sick, bind up wounds, stanch blood, alleviate pain, and lull to sleep; quench fire, allay the sea-storm, bring rain and hail; to burst bonds, undo chains and bolts, open mountains or close them up, and unlock treasures; to forward or delay a birth; to make weapons strong of soft, dull the edge of a sword; loop up knots, loose the bark off a tree , spoil a crop; call up evil spirits and lay them, to bind thieves...The Rûnatal, Sæm. 28-30, specifies eighteen effects of runes."
Grimm, Teutonic Mythology

Runes, used both for divination and for magic, are controversial in modern Heathenry. There are some who feel that using them is outside Norse practice or paganism, although, as the quote I used to open this section is meant to show, there is a historic basis for their use, particularly in magic. Runes are mentioned in Norse and Germanic myth in connection to magic fairly often and explicitly. The challenge isn't so much proving that they were used historically but that the evidence we do have for them, while clearly talking about what we consider runes, is often vague on exactly what symbol is being used for what purpose and the exact meanings ascribed to each one. As Grimm says in his Teutonic Mythology:

The olden time divided runes into many classes, and if the full import of their names were intelligible to us, we might take in at one view all that was effected by magic spells. (Grimm, 1888).

The evidence supports the magical use of runes by painting or carving the symbol onto various materials or even the human body, with the intention of the energy of the symbol then bringing about the desired result. Grimm tells us:

They were painted, scratched or carved, commonly on stone or wood, 'run-stones, runstaves'; reeds served the same purpose." (Grimm, 1888).

There are a series of runic symbols preserved in Icelandic grimoires of the 17th and 18th centuries usually with explicit instructions on how they were to be inscribed and onto what in order for their purpose to be achieved. An older example comes from Egil's Saga where Egil carves a rune on a drinking cup which contains a poisoned drink and chants over it causing the cup to burst. The Sigdrifumal lists a series of runes and their uses, including carving Tiwaz twice on the hilt of a weapon for victory:

> 6. Winning-runes learn, if thou longest to win,
> And the runes on thy sword-hilt write;
> Some on the furrow, and some on the flat,
> And twice shalt thou call on Tyr. (Sigdrifumal)

The text also discusses ale runes to carve on a drinking horn and the backs of your hands, with so-called "need" runes scratched on the fingernails, to keep other's from betraying you. Birth runes are drawn on the palms of the hands and around the joints if you are helping a woman in childbirth, with prayers to the fates for additional help. Sail runes must be carved on the prow and helm of a ship and burned into the oars for safety at sea. Branch runes are used, drawn on bark and leaf, to aid in healing, Speech runes are used for eloquence, and Thought runes for wisdom.

The difficulty here is deciding out of the runes that we have today which ones would be a wave rune or a thought rune. Every modern author will have their own opinions about what makes the most sense for each use and the reader should keep in mind that there is no right or wrong here, only opinions. While there is general agreement on Naudhiz being the need rune and in the poem, Tyr is explicitly referenced in relation to sword hilts, there is less agreement on branch runes or speech runes; certainly there was variation a thousand years ago as well just as there are various opinions today.

There are also some later 17th and 18th century Icelandic grimoires which feature runes and a type of symbol called a rune stave for magical purposes. Some of the more famous of these rune staves are the Aegishelm, which is said to convey invincibility, and the Vegvisir which protects during travel. Many of these from the grimoires include very specific means of production, such as carving on a specific type of wood, and an accompanying chant; these chants are often heavily Christianized due to the period they were written in.

Moving away from strictly magical uses we also find runes used for divination, both historically and today. As with the magical use the difficulty is that while we have solid evidence that runes were used for divination, we don't know what runes were used nor what symbolism was attached to each one; the modern systems that have been created are entirely modern even when they are based off of older sources.

While controversy continues over the use of runes for divination in favour of using runes this way, we do have this from the Havamal:

> *Hidden Runes shalt thou seek and interpreted signs, many symbols of might and power.*

We also have Tacitus discussing the Germanic tribes in Gaul and saying:

> *For auspices and the casting of lots they have the highest possible regard. Their procedure in casting lots is uniform. They break off a branch of a fruit-tree and slice it into strips; they distinguish these by certain runes and throw them, as random chance will have it, on to a white cloth. Then the priest of the State if the consultation is a public one, the father of the family if it is private, after a prayer to the gods and an intent gaze heavenward, picks up three, one at a time, and reads their meaning from the runes scored on them. If the*

lots forbid an enterprise, there can be no further consultation that day; if they allow it, further confirmation by auspices is required.
Tacitus, Germania

While it is highly unlikely that the lots mentioned in this passage featured any runes as we know them today, we can, however, conclude from this that some form of runes were used as far back as two thousand years ago for divination. The description shows that the process was treated very seriously and used for important matters. We also see that in Germania, wood from a fruit tree was used and the runes were prepared fresh before each use. The exact ritual described could be used by people today if they chose to stick to a more historic approach but modern runes would be needed.

Today runes are used for divination and generally the meanings are based on the old rune poems from Iceland, Norway, and Anglo-Saxon England. These can be found online or in Diana Paxson's book 'Taking Up the Runes' and while they were likely originally a mnemonic device for learning the alphabet (or futhark as it were) they offer insight into things associated with each runic symbol. These associations can be expanded out into meanings that can be associated with the rune for use in divination. There are also many good books on the market today that offer ideas and share the author's insight into possible divinatory meanings of each rune, although some stay much closer to the older sources than others.

According to the Havamal, Odin was the one who found the runes and brought them not only to humans but to the Aesir, Jotuns, Álfar, and Dvergar. The text tells us in detail how this was accomplished:

137. I trow I hung on that windy Tree
nine whole days and nights,
stabbed with a spear, offered to Odin,

myself to mine own self given,
high on that Tree of which none hath heard
from what roots it rises to heaven.
138. None refreshed me ever with food or drink,
I peered right down in the deep;
crying aloud I lifted the Runes
then back I fell from thence.
139. Nine mighty songs I learned from the great
son of Bale-thorn, Bestla's sire;
I drank a measure of the wondrous Mead,
with the Soulstirrer's drops I was showered.
140. Ere long I bare fruit, and throve full well,
I grew and waxed in wisdom;
word following word, I found me words,
deed following deed, I wrought deeds.
141. Hidden Runes shalt thou seek and interpreted signs,
many symbols of might and power,
by the great Singer painted, by the high Powers fashioned,
graved by the Utterer of gods.
142. For gods graved Odin, for elves graved Daïn,
Dvalin the Dallier for dwarfs,
All-wise for Jötuns, and I, of myself,
graved some for the sons of men."
(Bray, 1908)

Galdr

Galdr is the practice of using runes in spoken charms, songs, or chants. A single rune or a series of runes, even a rune poem, may be chanted in order to invoke a specific energy. The word galdr means to sing and represents a kind of sung magic originally, although in modern reconstructed practices the method is often closer to intoning than singing. Jolly explains it best here:

Words were channels of power; chanting or singing words added a special element of rhythm and controlled tone that gave even more power to the words. (Jolly, 1996, p 99)

Healing

Healing was an inherently magical practice for the pre-Christian and conversion era Heathens in my opinion, usually combining the use of herbs and stones with specific chants and spells. We can find examples in the Anglo-Saxon leechbooks of a variety of methods to heal everything from fevers to aelf[17] possession. Jolly argues persuasively in 'Popular Religion in Late Saxon England' that the written prayers or incantations associated with healing recipes in the leechbooks were always meant to be utilized through galdr, with the chanted prayers adding force to the herbal concoctions.

Cursing

Although it raises some sticky modern ethical dilemmas for some people, and is guaranteed to start a fight in most social media groups, cursing can be found in all (to my knowledge) ancient cultures. Norse cursing has its own distinct flavor that makes for an interesting subject to look into, and for our purposes here is an important aspect of Norse magic to understand.

Possibly one of the most well-known types of Norse curses, at least within Heathen groups, is the nidstang. A nidstang, or nithstong (scorn-post) is a 9-foot-long pole carved with runes that curse a specific person and topped with a severed horse's head or skull (Pennick, 1993). The basic idea of such a pole was to disturb or enrage the landvaettir in such a way that they turned the luck of the target of the curse bad (Pennick, 1993). Nidstangs could also be used to desecrate an area, in which case they were called alfreka, meaning to drive away the elves, with the understanding that to drive away the land spirits was to make the area spiritually impotent (Pennick, 1993). Nidstangs were also combined with curse-runes, where certain runes such as Thurisaz were carved a specific number of times in order to negatively affect the targeted person. In Egil's saga, Egil places a curse upon the king and queen who have made him an outlaw by erecting a nidstang and reciting a verbal curse to deny the spirits of the land rest until they force the king and queen out of the country.

Modern digital nidstangs containing a written curse exist online and have been used for such diverse purposes as cursing negative groups that have co-opted heathen symbols to cursing the perpetrators of the 9/11 terrorist attacks. Such a digital curse would work in a different fashion from the traditional poles, unless the caster believes there are digital or virtual wights that can affect the person and aims at turning them against the target. I would say that this type of modern nidstang is aimed more at making a bold public statement or damaging the target's reputation.

Part of the ritual associated with the nidstang includes spoken or chanted curses and we also see these separately, sometimes used with the invocation of runes. In the Curse of Busla, for example, we see both types as Busla attempts to use witchcraft to save her condemned son by cursing the king, after confronting him as he slept. First, she chants a long curse, which includes the verse:

> Shall trolls and elves and tricking witches,
> shall dwarfs and etins burn down thy mead-hall —
> shall thurses hate thee and horses ride thee,
> shall all straws stick thee, all storms stun thee:
> and woe worth thee but my will thou doest (Hollander, 1936)

When the king is still not willing to fully pardon her son, she continues with the final and most powerful verse:

> Come here six fellows: say thou their names:

56

I shall show them to thee unshackled all.
But thou get them guessed as good me seemeth,
shall ravening hounds rive thee to pieces,
and thy soul sink to hell-fire!" (Hollander, 1936).

After reciting the curse she draws specific runes in a pattern. Only after this does the king relent and Busla removes the curse she has just laid on him.

Similar to this we see another type of curse that was spoken but relied on verbally invoking specific runes. One version of this type of curse that I find particularly entertaining to study is the fretrunir, or farting curse. A father and son in Iceland were executed in 1656 after being convicted of using this curse against a pastor and a local girl in what is known as the Kirkjubol witch trial. Part of the chant that they used was said to be:

which are to afflict your belly with great shitting and shooting pains, and all these may afflict your belly with very great farting. May your bones split asunder, may your guts burst, may your farting never stop, neither day nor night. May you become as weak as the fiend, Loki, who was snared by all the gods. (Medievalist, 2019)

Clearly the intent is not only to humiliate the person with excessive gas but also to cause serious health problems relating to the stomach, intestines, and bowels. Another version from the Galdrbok includes the runes used and invokes an array of Heathen and Christian Powers, clearly with the same intent as the Kirkjubol example:

I write you eight áss-runes, nine naudh-runes, thirteen thurs-runes — that they will plague thy belly with bad shit and gas, and all of these will plague thy belly with great farting. May it loosen thee from thy place and burst thy guts; may thy farting never stop, neither day or night; thou wilt be as weak as the fiend Loki, who was bound by all the gods; in thy mightiest name Lord, God, Spirit, Shaper, Odhinn, Thorr, Saviour, Frey, Freyja, Oper, Satan, Beezlebub, helpers, mighty god, warding with the companions of Oteos, Mors, Notke, Vitales. (Lawless, 2010)

There are also examples of rune staves used for cursing, generally by carving the runic symbol on an object such as a piece of wood or bone and then placing it in the path of the target. Several of these types of rune staves can be seen in the Museum of Icelandic Sorcery and Witchcraft such as the killing rune which is intended to kill livestock belonging to the target. Those who study runes in modern practice also have found that certain runes used on their own can be effective curses, generally aimed at disrupting a person's luck or negatively impacting things around them or their health.

Chapter 7

Taking it Home

One's own house is best, though small it may be;
each man is master at home;
though he have but two goats and a bark-thatched hut
'tis better than craving a boon.
- Havamal

Ultimately you may do what you wish with the material in this book, but ideally it is meant to serve as a basis for understanding Heathenry and potentially applying that understanding to one's own spirituality. For those who would like to move further into such practice there is an appendix at the end of the book listing resources for further study.

It's important to remember that Heathenry is a diverse spiritual movement and while there are some broad strokes shared across all forms, no one can speak for the entire movement nor are there universal beliefs or practices. What follows in this chapter, as we wrap up Part I and head into part II discussing the Gods and spirits, is my personal suggestions for people who are interested in moving forward with this spirituality. In no way am I presenting this as authoritative, but I do hope that it may help readers with some of the final nuances.

Values

Because of the diversity of modern Heathenry there are not, necessarily, any values that are shared by every single group and individual following the Norse gods. You will see the Nine Noble Virtues mentioned frequently, but because their origin is controversial[18] not every group or individual acknowledges them. This section is going to look at the most common values that are often found across multiple Heathen belief systems, but it should be understood there will undoubtedly be exceptions.

1. Hospitality – a key aspect to both historic Heathenry as well as modern practice is hospitality, or the idea that it is important to be both a good host and a good guest.
2. Reciprocity – reciprocity is a vital aspect of Heathenry. It is believed that all things require a response and that balance is important. If you get a gift you should give a gift.
3. Responsibility – Heathens tend to strongly emphasize the idea of personal responsibility. If you make oaths you must keep them. You should deal honestly with friends, and repay those who help you. You must own your mistakes and strive not to repeat them.
4. Courage – facing life bravely is something that is encouraged and valued in Heathenry.

Words to the Wise: Racism and Ancestry

Norse Paganism is a beautiful and fulfilling path, but one with a history marred by several problematic things, which any seeker must be aware of. It is an unfortunate reality that to engage with the Heathen community or research modern Heathenry is to run headlong into a morass of racism and white supremacy and while that shouldn't deter people interested in the Norse gods it is important to be aware of. Several of the runes were used by the Nazi party in Germany and some are still used by neo-Nazis and white nationalists today, which has resulted in their placement on the USA's Southern Poverty Law Center's list of hate symbols. In the same vein some groups choose to use the Norse Gods as symbols of hate or to justify their own exclusionary prejudices.

The truth is that while modern Heathenry can be a mine field of white supremacy there is no basis in historic heathenry, mythology, or historic Norse culture to justify such mindsets. The Vikings were explorers who by various accounts took wives from other cultures in raids and settled in foreign lands.

Many people are drawn to Heathenry, and other types of cultural paganisms, because of an interest in ancestry. There is nothing wrong with seeking spirituality by looking to where you or your family has come from. However, it's important not to see that genetic connection as a free pass. What makes you a Norse pagan isn't who your great-grandmother was but how much you work to understand that culture and its Gods & spirits. Connection to these cultures takes effort and a willingness to be open minded and to learn.

I also encourage people to really think about why they are emphasizing this ancestral connection. Are you seeking to connect to spirituality through the guidance of ancestors? Or are you using ancestry as a way to feel entitled to a spirituality? Is that ancestral connection a stepping stone forward for you, or is it a shortcut to a sense of belonging?

Most importantly, do you think that people with no ancestral connection can still follow the Norse Gods? You don't need a DNA test to follow the Norse Gods. You just need a willingness to learn and connect to the specific culture, its beliefs, Gods, and practices.

Living Heathenry[19]

The most common question I am asked in relation to modern Heathenry is how does one begin? What follows is, of course, only my own opinion but I think it is good advice for anyone seeking to begin following this path.

1. Read the mythology, folklore, and stories to become familiar with the Gods and Spirits (Álfar/Dvergar/ assorted spirits) of the specific Heathen culture you are drawn to. Use this to get to know these Powers and to

start to understand the worldview and cosmology. You can't read too much of this stuff, ever, but always keep it in perspective for what it is and avoid the trap of fundamentalism.

2. Learn about your own ancestors and connect to them, whoever they are. The dead never truly leave us unless we forget them. Tell their stories, honor their memories, ask them for guidance and help in your life.

3. Respect the wights[20] of the land and your home. Learn about how the wights were and are understood and honored by the Heathen culture you are drawn to - be it Norse, Germanic, or Anglo-Saxon - and find ways to do this in your own life.

4. Be an honorable person. Live a life that reflects the values you want to embrace, including honesty, trustworthiness, loyalty, and courage. If you give your word, keep it. If you commit to something, see it through. Take responsibility for your own life, the good and the bad; be proud of your accomplishments and be willing to make amends for your errors.

5. Embrace reciprocity. Give as much as you get and seek balance between what you take and what you give.

6. Following along with point 5 - offer to the Gods, ancestors, and wights to create reciprocity with these Powers. Offer in thanks and celebration, for blessing and protection. Offerings create a relationship between us and the Powers we honor that is important in our spirituality.

7. Connect to your spirituality regularly by celebrating holidays, reading, and essentially living your faith. Heathenry isn't an occasional religion that you practice once in a while or a hobby, it's a way of life.

8. Set aside some space, no matter how small, in your home to honor the Gods. Think about who the Gods are to you, and what part they play in your life. Which Gods

do you connect most strongly to and why? Who do you honor most often? While each Heathen culture has its own pantheon you will find that within the pantheon there will be a selection of deities - perhaps as few as three or four, perhaps as many as a half dozen or more - that you are particularly drawn to for a variety of reasons. Over time these Gods will be the ones who you form the strongest connections to, much as each historic community had specific Gods within the wider pantheon that they honored.

A good first step to actively engaging with Heathenry is to look at ways to connect to ancestors, house spirits, and land spirits, as mentioned in point 3 above. I'll briefly expand on some suggestions on how to do that for those interested.

My initial approach to ancestor worship was to create an ancestor altar. At first this served simply as a way to feel connected to my ancestors who I had not known in life. However, as relatives who I knew and loved began passing away the purpose shifted to a place I could go and talk with them, light candles for them, burn incense, and leave offerings. My first ancestor altars were simple affairs, a small collection of pictures of my relatives, eventually with a simple white candle. Other Heathens prefer to visit the graves of their ancestors, believing that the dead stay where they are buried.

As time went on the altar grew and became more complicated, with a decorated resin skull being added to represent all of my ancestors whose names I did not know, but who were still with me in some sense. I also added a collection of small female statues to represent my Dísir, the female ancestors who guard my family line. Many of the pictures acquired little tokens or mementos, usually objects owned by that person in life, and more candles were added. In short, the altar developed its own personality.

So long as we remember those who have gone before us, whose lives gave us life, they are never really gone. They are our roots, our connection all the way back to the beginnings, and knowing them means knowing ourselves, who we are and where we came from. Even nameless, even unknown they are still there. I believe they can hear us when we speak to them and that they care about what happens to us, especially those people who loved us in life (blood relations or not). As long as I feel like they are there and care, I will be here, caring, speaking to them, and pouring out offerings for them.

There are some basic ways to connect to the helpful spirits in your home. I will give a short guide here.

- Keep things tidy – while a lot of folklore deals with house spirits like brownies who are reputed to clean up around a person's home (and wouldn't that be nice!) most house spirits and fairies more generally prefer people who are neat. There are many stories of those who were rewarded for keeping their homes clean and those who were punished for being messy. If you want happy house spirits, being tidy goes a long way.
- Create a space for them – this doesn't have to be large or fancy, but setting aside some small area for your house spirit to claim is a great way to let them know you welcome their presence.
- Leave out offerings for them – this is something we see across different cultures and traditions. Usually the offerings are left out rather unceremoniously, as house spirits are reputed to be shy and dislike too much direct attention. Offerings might include milk or cream, fresh bread, porridge with butter (on top), or sweets.
- Talk to them – house spirits can be reclusive and you may or may not see or sense yours but you can always talk to them. Make sure to always speak well of them – don't

even jokingly say anything rude or negative – and praise them if you feel like they are being helpful in any sense. If you want them to communicate back to you, I suggest asking for messages in dreams, it's a traditional approach and often effective.

Similar to house spirits, there are a few basic ways to begin connecting to the land spirits around you.

- Respect their places – if you want to connect to the land spirits anywhere the best start to is to show respect for that place. Most of this is common sense: don't litter, don't kill or destroy needlessly, don't speak ill of the place or it's spirit.
- Leave it better than you found it – I've found a great way to connect to land spirits is to clean up the ridiculous amounts of human flotsam and jetsam to be found. And if you think you won't find any whether you're in your neighbourhood, a state park, or a far of travel destination, trust me you will find plenty. There's human made garbage at the bottom of the deepest ocean trench and I have never gone anywhere, excluding perhaps some places in Iceland, that I haven't seen rubbish scattered around. Bring a bag with you and be ready to pick up any trash you find and the land spirits will appreciate it. (I have a more in-depth guide for pagans visiting sacred sites here)
- Accept that sometimes the answer will be no – a part of connecting to land spirits is understanding that they won't all like you and that's okay. If you feel unwelcome in a place, just politely leave.
- Offerings can also be an option with land spirits but I find they generally prefer things like clean water or local fruits. If you want to make offerings to these spirits it is

very important to consider what is safe to leave out that won't harm local plant and wildlife or create wider issues – no foreign seeds that might take root and grow, no milk poured out on plants (it will cause mould to grow), no food that could poison animals like chocolate, etc.

- Try to understand their perspective – land spirits have a very different perspective than humans do. One good way to connect to them is to try to understand that perspective. They are, I think, the souls of places and natural features and so they are tied to those places and things. They exist on an almost continuous scale; they change but they don't ever move from where they are rooted. They may be grand – a mountain – or humble – a small stream – but they are so long lived and so permanent-yet-always-changing. They feel but not as growing, living incarnated beings do. They think but in a different way.

And there you have it. You can add seeking community in real life or online as well, but I think that the heart of Heathenry starts with you and your own life. If you aren't a Heathen in your own life then all the community participation in the world won't make you one. That isn't to downplay the importance of community, which is a wonderful source of support, but if you can't be a Heathen without a community then you are missing the point altogether.

Chapter 8

Gods & Goddess

The Norse Gods and Goddesses are collectively known as the Aesir; this is also the term for the Gods specifically with the Goddesses called the Asynjyr. It is best to understand the groupings of the Norse Gods in a rather fluid way, with deities who were born as other types of beings, including Jotuns and Alfs, being considered Aesir if they married into the pantheon or were otherwise accepted into the group. The goddess Skadhi is one example of this, a Jotun who married into the Aesir and was later listed among the Aesir themselves. There are also three members of the rival group of Gods the Vanir who are considered Aesir because they were given as hostages to peace and live among the Aesir: Njord, Freya, and Freyr.

Some Norse deities were better preserved in written sources and folklore than others, so the following section will reflect the amount of material that we have for each deity. That said there is also a limit to how much material can be included in a book of this size, where a deity like Odin can and does have entire books focused on him. This text will try to cover the most important information on each deity and hopefully provide resources for further research.

The next point to be kept in mind is that the Norse pantheon as we have it today does not reflect the various groupings of Gods as they would have been known throughout the Norse world historically. The modern pantheon is a construction that has been pieced together from evidence across all of these diverse related cultures but the evidence doesn't always support all of these deities being acknowledged within the same area. Additionally some of the deities listed here, while receiving active veneration today, may not have had such worship historically and some scholars speculate that a few of them may have been purely literary inventions. At this point all of the deities being included are acknowledged and honoured in various ways today, whatever their origins.

When Snorri offers his famous list of the Norse pantheon in the Prose Edda, he divides the deities into two groupings: the Aesir [Gods] and Asynjyr [Goddesses]. Instead of adhering to such stark division by gender here I am going to list the various deities in three groupings: those traditionally understood to be included among the Aesir, the deities referred to as part of the Vanir, and those who are acknowledged as gods receiving worship or otherwise significant Powers but who don't easily fit into either of the two previous groupings. All of these divisions are artificial of course and should not be viewed as rigid separations. The deities will also be presented alphabetically by name.

Aesir

The gods of the Norse are a diverse group, encompassing both popularly worshipped deities as well as more obscure beings we know of from stories. In the following section I will try to offer a brief overview of the known Aesir and a quick description of each one.

Baldur

Balder's name in Old Norse is Baldr and he seems to have been an important deity originally. The son of Odin and Frigga, he is married to the goddess Nanna with whom he has a son, Forseti. Snorri describes him in the Gylfaginning in glowing terms as a beautiful, shining god whom everyone loves and who is the wisest, friendliest, and most well-spoken.

His particular home in Asgard is Breiðablik, which means 'the far shining one' (Simek, 1995) Snorri describes it as a place without impurity.

Baldur appears in a few key tales, particularly Baldrs Draumar or 'Balder's Dreams', which describes how Balder was suffering from repetitive dreams predicting his death; Odin seeks out a seeress who answers his questions about the dreams. Snorri includes the tale of Balder's death in his Prose Edda where we find that the gods sought to prevent what had been foretold and ended up bringing it about instead. Baldur is killed by the one item, a dart of mistletoe, to which he is vulnerable and goes to Helheim where he is given an enthusiastic welcome. The Voluspa suggests that Baldur will return after Ragnarök.

There have been several different interpretations of Baldur's death story, each of which colours how a person may relate to him and understand his place in the scheme of things. Some see parallels with the story of Christ's death and resurrection, while those who follow the ideas of Frazer's Golden Bough might see the story of a vegetation deity dying and being reborn, and others, notably de Vries, suggest the story reflects an initiation rite (Simek, 1993).

Bragi

An obscure god who may be the deification of a renowned 9th century poet of the same name. References to Bragi in stories are few and often seem to conflate a deity of that name with the mortal poet of the same name (Simek, 1993). Bragi's name is said by Snorri to be the source of the word for poetry, bragr, and he is generally understood as a god of that craft. Snorri describes Bragi as wise, eloquent, and skilled at poetry. His wife is the goddess Idunna.

Eir

Listed among the Aesir, Snorri refers to Eir as a goddess of healing. Her name means 'the helper' (Simek, 1993). A similarly named being appears as a Jotun's serving girl and as the name of a Valkyrie, although it's unclear if this is one personage or several similarly named ones.

Forseti

The son of Balder and Nanna, he is described as a god who adjudicates disagreements and is strongly connected to the law. There have been some suggestions that Forseti was a later creation, however, Simek argues persuasively that there is evidence of an 8th century island named after him as the eponymous deity worshipped by the people there.

Forseti's hall is Glitnir, which means 'shining one' and Snorri describes it as made of gold and silver (Simek, 1993).

Frigga

The pre-eminent goddess of the Norse pantheon is Frigga, whose name may mean 'beloved'. Friday is named after her, Freitag from Friatac in Old High German and Frigedaeg in Old English, both meaning Frigga's Day. She is the daughter of an obscure god, Fjorgynn, who shouldn't be confused with the similarly named goddess Fjorgyn, mother of Thor. She is the wife of Odin and mother of Baldur and is also known for having certain handmaidens, notably Fulla and Gná. Like Odin it is said that she sees the fates of all men, but unlike her spouse she doesn't speak of what she sees.

Frigga is often associated with domesticity and running the home; she is also likely a sovereignty goddess. Evidence of this is found in a story where Odin leaves for a time and his two brothers, Vili and Vé, rule in his absence. Until his return both of his brothers not only act as king together but sleep with Frigga[21], indicating that rulership may come through her.

There is sometimes confusion between Frigga and Freya[22] because of the various forms their names take in different places; in Germany Frigga is Freia or Frija, for example, which many people mistake for Freya's name although the two names, while similar share different roots; Germanic Freya would be something closer to Frowe.

One of the most well-known incidents featuring Frigga in myth is also indicative of her character more generally. Her son Baldur begins to have disturbing dreams and seeking an answer to them Odin travels to Helheim to talk to a dead seeress. He learns that Baldur is going to die and when he returns and relates this to the rest of the Aesir, Frigga sets out to stop it from happening. She travels the realms getting everything to promise not to harm Baldur, excluding only the mistletoe which she judged harmless. Baldur is subsequently killed by a dart of mistletoe, after Loki carves and hands the dart to Baldur's blind brother Hoðr having learned of this one weakness from Frigga. Mourning her son, Frigga gets Odin's son Hermod to make the journey to Helheim to ask if Hel would agree to let Baldur go, as she had absolute power over her realm; she did not want to free him and finally agreed to do so only if every living thing would weep for him. Everything did save one female Jotun[23] who refused, saying that Hel should keep what was hers.

Fulla

Fulla is described by Snorri as Frigga's handmaiden and one of the Aesir. Snorri describes her a maiden with long, loose hair and a golden headband and says she keeps some of Frigga's personal possessions. She may be identical to Volla found in some Anglo-Saxon lore.

Gefjon

Gefjon, also spelled Gefjun or Gefion, is listed among the Aesir in the Prose Edda. In the Heimskringla we are told that Gefjon had four sons with a Jotun, all of whom had the form of oxen. The Prose Edda tells us that when she travelled to Sweden the king there offered her as much land as she could claim by plowing with a team of oxen in 24 hours in exchange for her sexual favors; Gefjon agreed but brought her four oxen from

Jotunheim to plow the land, the implication being that the oxen were her sons. According to both sources they plowed so fast and deep that they separated nearly 3,000 square miles from the mainland creating a lake in Sweden and the island of Saelland which they dragged to Denmark.

In the Prose Edda, Gefjon is said to be a virgin deity who all women who die maidens go to after death. While the idea that maidens go to her when they die may be true, the assertion that Gefjon herself is a virgin is contradicted in the Poetic Edda and Heimskringla which both claim Gefjon was either married or had a lover. In the Lokasenna in the Poetic Edda when Loki challenges Gefjon he accuses her of trading her sexual favours to a young man for a necklace[24]; the Heimskringla says not only that she had the four aforementioned sons with a Jotun but also that she was married to an obscure son of Odin named Skjöldr.

Gerd

A female Jotun, Gerd is the daughter of Gymir, wife of Freyr and mother to his son Fjolnir. Snorri lists her as one of the Aesir. Simek sees her as an earth goddess and discusses theories that suggest her as either a force of civilization or of fertility of the land, paired with Fryer as a sun god[25].

The most well-known story of Gerd comes from the Skirismal, which tells of Freyr seeing Gerd from a distance, while sitting on Odin's high seat, and falling in love with her. He sends his servant to ask for her hand in marriage. Gerd initially refuses and a series of back and forth offers and threats are exchanged until she has no choice but to agree.

Gná

Found only in Snorri's Prose Edda list of the goddesses, Gná is said to be a messenger of Frigga who travels on a special horse that can fly through the air or run over water.

Heimdall

The meaning of Heimdall's name is unknown although Simek suggests 'one who illuminates', which may align with Snorri's description of him as 'the white god' who is *"great and holy"* (Simek, 1993). His other names or epithets are Gullintanni and Hallinskidi which mean 'gold teeth' implying that his teeth are either made of gold or seem like gold. He is the guardian of Asgard, gifted with keen eyesight and hearing, who protects the entrance to the realm. He needs very little sleep and keeps giants from invading the realm of the Aesir (Simek, 1993). He is the son of nine mothers, sometimes said to be sisters; in one version these are the nine daughters of Aegir usually assumed to be waves of the sea, while in another they are named as female Jotuns.

In several sources Heimdall is described as an ancestor of all humans. While Odin and his brothers created mankind Heimdall later went among humanity, using the name Rigr, and fathered children who are considered the ancestors of each of the social classes acknowledged by the Norse. He also taught humans important knowledge during his travels.

Heimdall lives in Himinbjorg near Bifrost; the name Himinbjorg may be understood as 'heaven's castle' (Simek, 1993). His horse is named Gulltopr or 'golden mane', further connecting him to gold, and his sword is Hofuð, or 'man's head' (Simek, 1993). His most famous possession may be the Gjallarhorn, 'loud sounding horn', which can be heard through the worlds and whose sounding will signal the beginning of Ragnarök (Simek, 1993).

Loki is Heimdall's enemy and the two are often shown at odds with each other. In the story of the theft of Freya's necklace Heimdall recovers the stolen item after fighting with Loki, who has taken it, both in the form of seals.

Hlín

Simek suggests that Hlín may simply be another name for Frigga but there did seem to be an established mythology about her by the turn of the first millennia, making it unclear if she is a unique deity or a by-name of Frigga. Her name means 'protector' and she seems to have been viewed as a deity of protection in general (Simek, 1993). Snorri says about her: "*she is established as keeper over those men whom Frigg desires to preserve from any danger.*"

Hoenur

A more obscure deity, Hoenur appears in the creation myth as one of Odin's brothers who helps create humans by giving them reason. He is the one who, along with Mimir, is given as a peace hostage to the Vanir. Hoenir listens to Mimir's wise advice in all things which makes the Vanir believe he himself is wise and so they make him a chieftain, only to realize later that Mimir is the wise one; in retaliation they kill Mimir, although Hoenir is left unharmed. He is referenced in several other stories but without any actual role in the action happening and he is said to be one of the Aesir who will continue after Ragnarök (Simek, 1993).

Hoðr

His names means warrior or fighter. Hoðr is the son of Odin and brother of Baldur who according to myth he kills, although the stories vary slightly in how that happens. In the Icelandic version Hoðr is blind and is given the fatal dart by Loki who then helps aim his throw; Loki is the one in that tale who takes the ultimate blame for Baldur's death, despite Hoðr's involvement. In Saxo's version, however, Hoðr, going by an alternate name, is a warrior who fights Baldur directly and is later killed for it (Simek, 1993). There has also been some speculative connection to a story contained within Beowulf where a man kills his brother in a tragic accident. In every version of the story the death is significant and Hoðr, whether by accident or design, is the key figure in bringing it about.

Idunna

Her name means 'the rejuvenating one' and she is the keeper of the apples which grant the Aesir immortality (Simek, 1995). Her parentage is unknown but her husband was Bragi. Her place among the Aesir is essential because of her role in keeping the gods young.

The only extant story of Idunna to survive into the modern era is one of her abduction by the Jotun Þjazi with Loki's help. The Aesir, beginning to age, force Loki to use Freya's falcon cloak to go into Jotunheim and retrieve Idunna, who he transforms into a nut and carries back. Þjazi chases him in the form of an eagle, only to be killed by the Aesir when he enters Asgard.

Lofn

As with many of the goddesses we find Lofn mentioned in Snorri's Edda and only once elsewhere so that little is known about her. Her name may mean either 'comforter' or 'the mild' (Simek, 1993). Snorri tells us that:

> she is so gracious and kindly to those that call upon her, that she wins Allfather's or Frigg's permission for the coming together of mankind in marriage, of women and of men, though it were forbidden before, or seem flatly denied.

Loki

Possibly the most often debated figure in Heathenry, Loki is often considered a trickster deity although his actual function is unclear. His name, similarly, is of uncertain meaning with several theories having been suggested which cannot be adequately substantiated. There are no proven locations connected to him or historic worship of him. Because of this wider uncertainty it is generally best to read the stories Loki appears in and draw your own conclusions about his nature.

Although Loki is the child of two Jotuns he is counted among the Aesir and is described as a blood brother to Odin. In the Lokasenna we learn that Odin has sworn never to drink unless Loki is served as well. Nonetheless Loki can be a controversial figure in Heathenry and Asatru where he is sometimes equated to a Devilish figure similar to the Christian Satan; in some groups it is anathema to mention his name in ritual or call on him. That view lacks all nuance, however, and is a gross oversimplification of Loki's actual role in the mythology.

Loki appears in many of the myths and as often as he causes the Aesir problems he also solves their problems and brings them gifts. When a Jotun approaches Asgard and offers to build a wall around it in exchange for Freya, the sun and moon if he can do it in a certain amount of time it is Loki who convinces the Aesir to agree; and when it looks like the Jotun will succeed because his horse is able to move great amounts of stone it is Loki who the Gods pressure into tricking him into failure. He does this by taking the form of a mare and luring the stallion away so that the Jotun can't finish his work in time. When Loki eventually returns to Asgard he brings his new offspring, an eight-legged foal named Sleipnir who will later become Odin's steed, with him.

While Loki is Sleipnir's mother he is also father to several children. With the female Jotun, Angrboda, he has Hel, Fenrir (a monstrous wolf), and Jormungandr (the world serpent) and with the Aesir goddess, Sigyn, he has two sons, Vali and Narfi. Loki's own mother is Laufey and his father is Farbauti, both Jotuns about whom little is known. In the Lokasenna Loki claims to have had affairs with Skadhi, Sif, and also fathered a son with Tyr's (unnamed) wife.

One of Loki's most well-known stories tells how he gained the Gods' greatest treasures. It began when he cut off all of Sif's hair[26] and Thor threatened his life, causing him to promise to replace the hair. He did this by going to the dwarves who he gets to compete to see who can make the most impressive treasure, with his own head as the prize. The dwarves make golden hair for Sif, Odin's spear Gungnir and arm ring Draupnir, Freyr's ship Skiðblaðnir and golden boar Gullinbursti, and Thor's hammer Mjolnir. Because Loki is unable to distract the dwarves and cause them to fail, he loses but convinces them not to take his head; instead his mouth is sown shut. This story also illustrates Loki's general role among the Aesir, where he often causes relatively minor problems but solves them in ways that greatly benefit the Gods.

Loki is Thor's main travelling companion in myth and described as a blood-brother of Odin and in general his stories align with this. He is often the source of strife but also of blessings for the Gods and it is only in the stories leading up to Ragnarök that he shifts into a more directly malevolent force. We see this with Baldur's death which Loki arranges and then in his actions during the Lokasenna where he arrives at Aegir's hall uninvited and begins insulting all present, leaving only when Thor arrives. He is eventually hunted down because of his role in Baldur's death, caught, and punished; his son Vali is turned into a wolf who kills his son Narvi and Loki is bound in a cave using his son's entrails. Skadhi hangs a venomous snake above him so that it drips on his face. His wife Sigyn stays by his side holding a bowl to protect him from the venom but when it fills and she must empty it the poison strikes him and he writhes in his captivity causing earthquakes. When Ragnarök arrives Loki fights against the Aesir on the side of the Jotuns.

Nanna

The wife of Baldur and Forseti's mother. The meaning of her name is unknown. The main story in which we see her is that of Baldur's death where she dies of grief mourning him and is burned with him on his funeral pyre, one assumes going with him to Helheim.

Odin

One of the most well-known Gods of the Norse pantheon, introduced in the Prose Edda as the most important of the Gods and given multiple different names, is Odin. While the Prose Edda material should be viewed carefully as a product of its time and with clear Christian influences – Odin for example is initially described in ways nearly synonymous to the Christian God – his overall importance particularly to kings and poets is clear. He is a complex and multifaceted deity known across the Norse world by various names including Odin, Oðinn, Wodan, and Woden which are all derived from the same root term, as well as hundreds of bynames, or heiti, which are usually descriptive in nature. These include Grimnir (hooded one), Alföðr (all father), Ganglari (wanderer), Hangatyr (god of the hanged), Hrafnagud (raven god) and Oski (wish granter) Sigfodur (victory father)[27]. Simek describes him as a god of poetry, the dead, war, magic, runes, and ecstasy, as well as the father of the gods which is in line with the wider modern understanding of who and what Odin is.

Odin is the son of the primordial being Buri and the female Jotun Bestla, and he along with his brothers Vili and Vé[28] created the worlds. Odin's wife is Frigga, although he is also known to have a multitude of lovers including Rind and the female Jotuns Skadhi, Griðr, Jord, and Gunnlod. Unsurprisingly he also has many children including Thor, Baldur, Vali, Hoðr, Vidar, Bragi, and possibly Tyr and Heimdall. Snorri in the Prose Edda claims that Odin is called the All Father because he is the literal father of all the Aesir and that he is the *"highest and oldest of all the gods"*. He is a deity of sovereignty and also of creation, being the literal creator of humans, with his two brothers, as well as the progenitor of several human family lines including the Volsungs and Anglo-Saxon royal lines (Simek, 1993).

He is the one who won the runes for the various beings, including those given to humans, by stabbing himself and hanging on the world tree for nine days and nights. He also sacrificed an eye to Mimir's well for wisdom, either to drink from the well or to gain counsel from Mimir's head which is preserved there. Much of Odin's nature seems to be focused on gaining wisdom and utilizing it and the stories he features in usually include this aspect, so that we see him for example going out to win the mead of poetry which is being kept by a Jotun or travelling to Helheim to consult with a dead seeress over the fate of his son Baldur. In contrast to Thor's heroic adventures, often defending mankind, Odin's stories include themes of acquiring knowledge or of seducing women; a stark comparison of the two deities can be seen in the Harbardsljod where the two trade barbs with Thor bragging of killing Jotuns and Odin of his amorous adventures.

Odin appears in many stories, and physical descriptions of him include both an older man as well as a younger one in his prime. He is most often described missing an eye, although which one isn't specified, so that he wears a hooded cloak or hat which cover that side of his face. Modern artistic depictions favour showing him as an older man with grey hair and wearing an eye patch.

His famous steed is Sleipnir an eight-legged horse who is the offspring of Loki and Sviðilfari (a stallion); Sleipnir is able to travel freely between all nine worlds. He has two ravens, Huginn and Muninn who travel the world and relay information to Odin, as well as two wolves, Geri and Freki, who consume his food. Odin also possesses the spear Gungnir and the arm ring Draupnir, made by the dwarves and considered treasures of the Aesir.

His home is Valhalla, the hall of the slain, where the dead heroes chosen by Odin's Valkyries live. These heroes feast in Odin's hall and fight in an endless cycle until Ragnarök when they will battle on the side of the Aesir against the Jotuns. In this hall Odin has a seat named Hlidskjalf from which he can see all things.

Odin is the Norse god of magic, known to practice seidr which he learned from Freya as well as using poetry and runes. His knowledge of seidhr is something that is mentioned mostly in a negative sense, a practice associated with women that Odin nonetheless also did; in the Lokasenna the two accusations Loki makes against Odin are that he gives victory unjustly and that he went among humans working female magic and in disguise as a woman. His use of poetry and runes for magic are well known and perhaps explain why Odin went to such lengths himself to gain both the mead of poetry as well as the runes. He uses magic in various ways in different stories including for healing and he is referred to as *"Father of the magic chant"* (Simek, 1993).

Odin has been connected to the Wild Hunt who are sometimes called Oensjaegeren (Odin's Hunters) or Odens Jakt (Odin's Hunt) and who in some areas Odin is said to lead [29] (Kershaw, 2000). Kershaw theorizes that the Wild Hunt and Odin's connection to it may reflect a very old tradition of initiation through or into a cult of Odin. This may or may not relate to Odin's role as a god of the dead, particularly the battle dead, which the Wild Hunt was associated with. In mythology Odin was given half the battle dead, sharing the other half with Freya. There are also references to beliefs that he could choose who would live or die in battle and who would win or lose, and in at least one account we see an opposing army being dedicated as offerings to Odin by having a spear cast over them. Besides the battle dead he had an association with those who were hanged, earning him the name God of the Hanged. He was also associated with a specific shade of blue that is thought to be the colour of corpses.

Sága

Her name has an uncertain meaning, possibly related to seeing, and little is known about her although she is referenced in several places. Her home in Asgard is Sokkvabekkr[30] [sunken bank]. She drinks with Odin in this hall and seems to have a protective role.

Sif

The wife of Thor and mother to the god Ullr; possibly (although not certainly) the lover of Loki. Her name means 'the wife' or 'related by marriage' and Simek suggests that she was a literary creation paired with Thor as he gained popularity. Whether or not this is so she is found in several of the myths and is well known in modern Heathenry today where she is usually associated with the harvest. The expression 'Sif's Hair' was used to mean gold, either because her hair was pictured as like gold or because of the story where Loki shears off her hair and replaces it with dwarven made hair of literal gold. There has been much speculation that her hair may also have been an analogy for corn or grain, although there is a type of moss named 'sif's hair' which may contradict this view (Simek, 1993).

Sigyn

The wife of Loki and mother of his sons Narvi and Vali, Sigyn is listed as one of the Aesir by Snorri, although little is known about her. Her name may mean 'victory friend' (Simek, 1993). Her main appearance in myth is in the story of Loki's punishment where we are told she stays by him after he is bound and uses a bowl to catch the poison dropping into his face.

Sjofn

Another obscure goddess, her role seems to primarily focus on love and marriage. Snorri has this to say about her: *"she is most diligent in turning the thoughts of men to love, both of women and of men."*

Skadhi

A female Jotun, Skadhi is accepted as one of the Aesir after marrying the god Njorð and is counted among their number afterwards. Her father is the Jotun Þjazi and her mother is unknown. After leaving Njorð she becomes one of Odin's lovers and the mother of some of his sons, notably earl Hákon, (Simek, 1993).

The story of Skadhi's inclusion into the Aesir is one of the more colourful ones in Norse myth. Skadhi's father, Þjazi, is killed by Thor and she goes to Asgard seeking vengeance. The Aesir suggest compensation instead and offer to let her marry any of their number with the only catch being that she must choose her new husband by his feet. She agrees to this and chooses the most beautiful pair of feet, wanting Baldr as her husband and assuming they must belong to him. Instead the beautiful feet belong to the sea god Njorð. As a second part of the compensation paid to her it is agreed that the Aesir must make her laugh – a daunting task. They have no success until Loki finally resorts to tying a rope around a goat's beard with the other end attached to his testicles; every time the goat tosses its head the rope is pulled and Loki jumps around, causing even the grim Skadhi to laugh.

Her marriage to Njorð is short lived, as he prefers to live in his seaside home and she prefers the mountains. Her home is Þrymheim [noisy home] a snowy mountainous place where she can ski and hunt; in the source material she is called a ski goddess and is described using a bow and arrow to hunt (Simek, 1993).

Besides Njorð and Odin, Skadhi also has a complicated relationship with Loki. He is the one who caused her father's death, yet he also makes her laugh as part of the payment she demands of the Aesir. In the Lokasenna he accuses her of going to his bed[31] yet when he is finally punished by the Aesir for his part on Baldur's death she is the one who hangs the venomous snake above his head. It is unclear from all of this where exactly the two stand with each other.

Snotra

Her names means 'clever one' and in the Edda she is called *"prudent and of gentle bearing"* but we know little else about her.

Syn

Her name means 'refusal' or 'denial' and was used in poetry in kennings for 'woman' (Simek, 1993). She clearly plays a protective role and Simek suggests that she may have originally been a Dísir or one of the matronae who was later included among the Aesir. Snorri tells us that Syn:

> *keeps the door in the hall, and locks it before those who should not go in; she is also set at trials as a defence against such suits as she wishes to refute.*

Thor

Perhaps the most popular God in the Norse pantheon is Thor, both today and historically. His name is related to the word for thunder and he is universally seen as a thunder god, as well as a deity of fertility, protection, and the average person. Thor has long been the God of the common person, so his wide spread popularity shouldn't be surprising and it was he, out of all the Norse Gods, who became the chief rival and opponent to Jesus during the conversion period. He is also pictured throughout his myths as the defender of humans against the forces of entropy embodied by the dangerous Jotuns. Thursday is named after him.

He is the son of Odin and the earth goddess Jorð, and through Odin the brother of many significant deities like Baldur. His wife is the goddess Sif and through her he is the stepfather of Ullr; he also has two sons, Magni and Moði, as well as a daughter, Þruðr. He has various female Jotuns as lovers. In his journeys through both Midgard and Jotunheim he is often accompanied by Loki, and less often by Tyr. He also has two human children who act as his servants, Þjálfi and Roskva, to repay him for laming one of his goats when he was a guest of their parents.

Thor's home in Asgard is called Þrudheim, 'strength home', and his hall is Bilskírnir. According to Odin's accusation in the Harbardsljod the common people who die go to Thor's hall. He is well established as a patron of the common man, in contrast to Odin as god of kings and poets, so this may well represent genuine belief. Thor himself is pictured as a large, strong man, usually red bearded, with a quick temper. Despite his often-oafish depiction in stories he is also very clever as we see in the story where he contests in a battle of wits the Dvergar Alvis [literally All Wise] over the hand in marriage or Thor's daughter; Thor wins by keeping the dwarf talking until the sun rises and he is turned to stone.

Thor's main method of travel is by goat-drawn chariot, earning him the names chariot god and lord of goats; his goats are named Tanngrisnir and Tanngnjóstr (Simek, 1993). These are not normal goats but rather are supernatural beings who can be killed and eaten one night and will resurrect the next day. This ability is a key feature in the story of how Þjálfi and Roskva end up as his servants, because when Thor warns them not to break any of the goats' bones when they are being eaten Þjálfi does so anyway to get to the marrow, resulting in the goat being lame the next day. The two children must serve Thor to repay this offense. Thor also has several items that add to his strength, given to him by the female Jotun, Griðr, including a staff, iron gauntlets and a belt which increases his strength.

Thor's most renowned possession is his hammer, Mjolnir, which was forged by the dwarves. It was an ideal weapon which he used to great effect against the Jotuns he fought, its only minor flaw being a short handle. During the conversion period Thor's Hammer would become a religious symbol, like the Christian cross, and it is still used as such today (Simek, 1993). Mjolnir was also used to bless brides on their wedding day, indicating a function for fertility. There are several stories where Thor's hammer is stolen by the Jotuns and Thor must regain it, in one case by fighting for it in another by tricking the Jotun who has taken it by pretending to be Freya.

Thor's greatest enemy is Jormungandr, the Midgard serpent, who is a child of Loki. Simek argues that this story is one of the oldest foundational tales of Thor, based on how widespread it is and the number of images found depicting their struggle with each other. We find one main tale of their encounters preserved today, in which Thor is out fishing with a Jotun and accidently hooks Jormungandr. He begins to pull up the serpent but the Jotun he is with cuts the line freeing it. We also are told in the Voluspa that Thor and Jormungandr will fight at Ragnarök and while Thor will kill the serpent he will be fatally wounded in the process.

Evidence for worship of Thor is abundant and widespread, undoubtedly a sign of his popularity. It has been popular in Iceland going back to the sagas for people to have names related to Thor and there is an account of a carved image of Thor being thrown overboard and followed to find a place for a community to settle. We also have numerous accounts of temples dedicated to Thor or of Christian saints destroying sacred statues of Thor, all of which point to the widespread nature of his worship. It is also significant, as has been touched on previously, that Thor was the main antagonist to Christ during the conversion period.

Tyr

Tyr is an ancient deity, traced back prior to the Norse period; Simek speculates that he existed during the Indo-European period as a sky god (Simek, 1993). It has been suggested that Tyr was originally the main god of the pantheon who was later displaced by Odin. This may perhaps explain why Tyr's importance as a god of war and oaths is often emphasized but he himself doesn't have a very active role in the mythology. The name Tyr is used not only as a personal name for this deity but also as a general term for 'god' so that we find. For example, one name for Odin is 'Hangatyr'. The plural of Tyr's name, tivar, means gods (Simek, 1993).

The most well-known story of Tyr explains the loss of his hand. The Aesir are raising Loki's son Fenrir, who is in the form of a great wolf. Tyr is the one brave enough to feed the wolf and when the gods decide to bind Fenrir, fearing the destructive power he could unleash, only Tyr is willing to put his hand in the wolf's mouth as a pledge that he will be freed. Of course he is not freed and takes the god's right hand off. As Simek says (quoting De Vries):

The myth of Tyr shows how a god wants to pay for the security of the cosmic order by telling a necessary lie which results in the loss of his hand (Simek, 1993, p 337).

We do not know much about Tyr's family; he isn't said to have a wife in the bulk of the mythology; although Loki claims in the Lokasenna to have fathered a son on Tyr's unnamed wife but she is mentioned nowhere else. One source suggests his father was the Jotun Hymir while another (Snorri) claims his father is Odin. At Ragnarök he will fight, kill, and be killed by Garm the guard dog of Helheim, although it has been suggested originally, he fought Fenrir, who had taken his hand, and only later shifted to fighting Garm when Odin took over the role of head of the pantheon.

In general Tyr is seen as a god of battle, with his name carved onto swords twice to ensure victory according to the Sigdrifumal, of justice, and possible of cosmic order. There is evidence of worship of Tyr historically particularly in Denmark and less so in Norway. The rune Tiwaz is strongly connected to Tyr and may also indicate his importance in earlier periods.

Ullr

Ullr is the son of Sif and stepson to her husband Thor; we don't know who his father is. He lives in Ydalir, yew valley, and is renowned for his winter skills including skiing and ice skating (Simek, 1993). He is described as a skilled archer as well as a deity called on in duels. His name is used in kennings for warriors and Simek describes his appearance as 'warlike'.

Vali

Odin's son[32] by Rind, who is alternately listed as one of the Aesir or a human princess. His conception is arranged through deception and spells by Odin who wants to fulfill a prophecy relating to avenging Baldur's death. Vali is referred to as Baldur's avenger and little else is known about him outside his appearance and actions within that narrative (Simek, 1993). According to Snorri he avenged Baldur's death when he was only one day old.

Vár

Vár, alternately Vór, is an obscure goddess whose name means 'beloved'. Snorri says of Vár that: *"she harkens to the oaths and compacts made between men and women"*. He describes her as a goddess of oaths and who punishes those who lie under oath. Simek considers her a goddess of marriage and of love and points out that in the Þrymskviða, Vár is called on to solemnize marriages (Simek, 1993).

Vé

An extremely obscure deity whose name means 'shrine'. In Snorri's version of the creation of the nine worlds Vé is one of Odin's brothers who helps him defeat the primordial Jotun, Ymir and fashion creation. In the Lokasenna, Loki accuses Frigga of sleeping with both Vé and Odin's other bother Vili when Odin was out wandering in the worlds.

Vidar

Odin's son with the female Jotun Griðr.[33] It is Vidar who will kill Fenrir at Ragnarök to avenge Odin's death. His home in Asgard is the eponymously named Vidarsland and he is one of the younger deities who will survive Ragnarök and go on to begin the new world afterwards. Snorri describes him this way in the Edda:

> *Vídarr is the name of one, the silent god. He has a thick shoe[34]. He is nearly as strong as Thor; in him the gods have great trust in all struggles.* (Brodeur, 1916).

Vili

Odin's brother and the brother of Vé, son of Bor and Bestla. Little is known about him but he acted with Odin to kill Ymir and to create the worlds. He also took over ruling the Aesir, with Vé, when Odin was travelling through the world and during that time had Frigga as his lover.

Vanir

The Vanir represent the second major grouping of Gods in Norse mythology although we only know about a small number of them in any detail. These few, however, represent some of the most popular and well-known deities in the entire pantheon, with one of them – Freyr – having a place beside Odin and Thor as the three main deities found in the temple at Uppsala Sweden.

The Vanic gods are associated with fertility, particularly of the land, and with good weather (Simek, 1993). Additionally, through Freya, they are associated with the kind of magic known as seidr. There is little existing mythology about the Vanir and most of what we know about them comes from their interactions with the Aesir and the period of time while Freya, Freyr, and Njorð are living in Asgard.

The Vanir are first encountered in the Prose Edda where we

learn that they were at war with the Aesir, a war that began when the Aesir impaled and burned the goddess Gullveig. Gullveig didn't die but was reborn under the name Heiðr, however, the attack was the opening volley in a war between the two groups of deities. The war lasted until peace was finally made with the exchange of hostages between the two groups. The Aesir sent Mimir and Hoenir to the Vanir and the Vanir sent Njorð and his two children Freyr and Freya to the Aesir. Hoenir relied on Mimir for good advice in order to seem wiser than he was and when the Vanir eventually realized this, they felt they had been duped in the exchange and decapitated Mimir, sending his severed head back to the Aesir (Simek, 1993). Despite this violence the peace held and the Vanic hostages remained among the Aesir.

Freya

Her name is derived from the word for 'Lady', lending itself to confusion in some source material. She is the daughter of Njorð and his unnamed sister, and has a brother Freyr. In the Lokasenna Loki accuses her of incest with her brother which she doesn't deny and Simek suggests that she may have originally been married to Freyr, possibly a custom of the Vanir. In the Eddas her husband is said to be Oðr and she has two daughters, Hnoss and Gersimi.

Despite coming from the Vanir and joining the Aesir by choice, because she followed her brother and uncle who were peace-hostages, Freya is arguably one of the most important of the Norse goddesses and one of the most popular today. She is a multifaceted deity who aids lovers who call on her and also receives a portion of the battle dead, who she divides with Odin, making her both a goddess of lovers and of battle. She is also more broadly associated with magic, particularly seidhr, and of fertility. In the Eddas many stories feature a Jotun or other chaotic being trying to steal or win Freya, often along with the sun and moon, indicating her primal importance.

Freya is known by a variety of alternate names including: Mardoll[35], Horn [flax], Gefn [giving one], Syr [sow] and Vanadis [Vanir woman] (Simek, 1993).

In Asgard her home is Folkvangir and her hall is Sessrumnir; Folkvangir means 'field of people' and Sessrumnir means a place with many seats (Simek, 1993). Both of these names emphasize the large numbers of people seemingly associated with Freya's home and hall, emphasizing perhaps her popularity or her role as host of half the battle dead. She also possesses a famous falcon cloak which allows the wearer to assume the form of a falcon as well as a chariot pulled by cats and a boar named Hildisvini, who in the story he appears in, is actually her human lover Ottar shape changed. She travels in the cat-drawn chariot and in one story rides the boar; it should be noted the cats referred to here are not domestic cats but probably wild cats or a similar animal that would have been referred to as a cat. Her most famous possession, however, is without doubt the necklace Brisingamen,[36] a renowned masterpiece created by four dwarves. To acquire this necklace Freya agreed to spend one night with each of the four after which they gave Brisingamen to her. The necklace features in a story that is found in several versions across multiple related cultures, where it is stolen often by Loki at Odin's behest; Loki and Heimdall then fight over the necklace, sometimes in the form of seals, before it is returned to Freya. In at least one version Odin only returns it when Freya agrees to incite a war among rival groups on earth.

Physical descriptions of Freya are uncommon but she is described as crying tears of gold or amber. This is mentioned in a story where we learn that her husband, Oð, has left and she is searching the world trying to find him. As she stands on the shore, she cries tears of gold, or alternately amber, which is how people explain finding amber near the shoreline.

There is limited evidence of actual worship of Freya historically, although she was beloved enough in Iceland that a poet was outlawed[37] after reciting a poem insulting the goddess at the All-Thing (Simek, 1993). There are multiple places named after her and at least one reference to her worship in myth; in the Hyndluljóð, Freya says that she is seeking answers for Ottar because he has made so many offerings at her altar that the stone looks like glass. Simek suggests that her main worship would have been in the home rather than the public sphere, to fit with her other associations with love and potentially as a guardian figure.

Freyr

His name means Lord, although he also called Froði, Fricco and Ingvi. Freyr is a complex deity, seen as the ancestor of the Yngling dynasty in Sweden and also associated with the Ljósálfar or light elves. It is said that Freyr received Ljósálfheim as tooth-gift and he is strongly associated with those beings who themselves show many features and powers similar to the Ljósálfar including control of the weather and fertility of crops. Simek in his 'Dictionary of Northern Mythology' additionally suggests that Freyr would have been a god of harbors and seafaring along with his father Njorð.

Freyr is the son of Njorð and his unnamed sister and has a sister named Freya; there has been some speculation that the two may be twins. In the Lokasenna, Loki claims that Freya and Freyr were lovers and Simek suggest that they were probably married prior to joining the Aesir, after which they each found different spouses (Simek, 1993). Freyr's wife according to the Eddas is the female Jotun, Gerðr, who he eventually wins after a serious of promises, threats, and the surrender of his sword. By one account he would fight instead with a deer's antler. His most famous possession is the gold boar Gullinbursti [gold bristles] who was created by a dwarf as one of the treasures of the Aesir (Simek, 1993).

Freyr is described this way by Snorri in the Gylfaginning:

Freyr is the most renowned of the Æsir; he rules over the rain and the shining of the sun, and therewithal the fruit of the earth; and it is good to call on him for fruitful seasons and peace. He governs also the prosperity of men. (Brodeur, 1916, p 38).

This reinforces the reasons for his widespread popularity, that is his connection to the success of crops, weather, and peace. Freyr, along with Odin and Thor, was one of three gods honoured at the temple in Uppsala Sweden. The statue there was said to have a giant phallus, indicative of Freyr's connection to fertility, which is also reflected in an Icelandic story of a priestess of Freyr who journeyed across the country with a statue of the god and eventually a man acting in the role of Freyr; it was taken as a good omen when she became pregnant (Simek, 1993).

In a euhemerized version of Freyr's life Snorri tells us that he was a Swedish king named Yngvi who ruled during a time of great peace and prosperity. When he died his royal court kept it secret for several years, during which his corpse was given the devotion and sacrifices usually seen with a divinity.

Multiple place names are attributed to Freyr, especially in eastern Sweden. There are also literary references to sacrifices made in honour of the God, establishing that he was definitely a fixture of Norse paganism. There is also documentation of oaths in Sweden taken in Freyr's name, usually in combination with Njorð, as well as rituals in Norway dedicated to Odin, Freyr, and Njorð (Simek, 1993). His cult is further established by the use of 'priest of Freyr' (Freysgoði) as a personal name and of accounts of a priest who carried a small image of Freyr with him (Simek, 1993).

Gullveig

An obscure being who is probably, but not certainly, one of the Vanir in the source material but is generally assumed to be among their number. Several scholars including Turville-Petre suggest that Gullveig is another name for Freya (Simek, 1993). This may or may not be true but there is clear overlap in their activities and characteristics.

Gullveig, whose name may mean 'gold greed' or 'gold power', is described in the Voluspa as a seeress. She is skewered in spears by the Aesir and burnt three times in Odin's hall in Asgard but each time she is reborn. This action begins the war between the Aesir and Vanir.

Heiðr

The name given to Gullveig after she is burned by the Aesir. Simek suggests it may mean 'fame' but also connects it to the same meaning of 'gold greedy' as Gullveig. According to the Voluspa Heiðr then travels around prophesying and using her magic and was a delight to so-called evil women, possibly a reference to her teaching or practicing seiðr with human women. The full description of Heiðr in the Poetic Edda is:

> Heith they named her who sought their home,
> The wide-seeing witch, in magic wise;
> Minds she bewitched that were moved by her magic,
> To evil women a joy she was

Njorð

A deity strongly associated with the ports and harbours, Njorð is the father of Freyr and Freya with his own unnamed sister; several scholars including Simek have suggested such sibling marriages may have been standard among the Vanir. He along with his two children go to the Aesir as a peace hostage and there he lives in Nóatún by the sea. His wife while he is among the Aesir is the female Jotun, Skadhi, although the marriage is not a successful one because he prefers to live by the water and she prefers the mountains. The name of Njorð's home, Nóatún, means 'place for ships', reinforcing his connection to harbours

(Simek, 1993).

Njorð is most well known as a deity of the harbour who fisherman and sailors looked to but according to Snorri he ruled over the sea, wind, and fire. Although there are very few surviving stories of Njorð in the mythology his previous popularity seems clear. There are many place names connected to him in Sweden and Norway; interestingly while the Norwegian locations are as expected coastal ones, the Swedish sites are generally inland causing some speculation that Njorð may have originally been a deity of agricultural fertility (Simek, 1993).

Miscellaneous

The main deities that are focused on in the Norse pantheon are members of the Aesir and their Vanic hostages, but the Aesir are not the only ones who are worshipped. There are also a small group of beings who are not counted among the Aesir but are given worship today and potentially historically as well. This is not an exhaustive list and there could be other beings that that might be included in worship by some people which do not appear here. I am focusing on the more well-known ones I am aware of.

Aegir

Aegir's name means 'sea' and that seems to be his main purview in the myths. Although people tend to immediately jump to Njorð when thinking of Norse sea gods, the Vanic deity is associated more with harbors than the open ocean; that would be the realm of Aegir and his wife Rán. His other two names, according to Snorri, are Hlér and Gymir, both of which also probably mean sea (Simek, 1993). This would likely place him in the ranks of other sea gods where he and his realm where somewhat synonymous with each other.

Although Aegir is counted among the Jotun-folk unlike many of the Jotuns he is on friendly terms with the Aesir. He has a great hall and is known for his hospitality. These feature heavily in the Lokasenna a story during which Loki comes into Aegir's hall uninvited while the Aesir are having a party, insults everyone present, and eventually sets the hall on fire.

Aegir's father is Fornjótr; some sources say that Rán is Aegir's daughter while others claim that Rán is his wife with whom he has nine daughters; the phrase 'Aegir's daughters' is used as a kenning for the waves of the sea (Simek, 1993). The view of Rán as his wife seems to be the more popular in modern Heathenry. His nine daughters are sometimes given specific names, which are often simply words meaning 'wave'.

Fenrir

Fenrir is the son of Loki and the female Jotun Angrboda and he is in the form of a great wolf. His main stories revolve around his being bound by the Aesir and his role in Ragnarök.

The Aesir raised him but as he grew, he became frighteningly strong so that they decided to bind him. The first two attempts failed because Fenrir easily broke through the strongest of ropes, so the Aesir went to the dwarves and asked them to make an unbreakable binding. To do this they took several non-existent things and wove them together: a woman's beard, spittle from a bird, the roots of a mountain, the sound of a cat's paw, and the breath of a fish. When the Aesir went to apply this, however, the wolf was suspicious as the binding didn't look like anything more than a ribbon and seemed odd after their previous attempts. He finally agreed to let them try to bind only if Tyr would place his hand in the Fenrir's mouth as a pledge of good will that he would be freed again. Tyr agreed and when Fenrir couldn't break the ribbon, he bit off the god's hand. The wolf was then tied to a boulder and had a sword placed in his open mouth so that he couldn't close it.

At Ragnarök he will break free and eventually kill Odin before being killed by Odin's son, Vidar. Simek also suggests that Fenrir may be synonymous with the hound of Helheim, Garm, that kills Tyr, as well as the wolf or wolves who consume the sun and moon at the start of Ragnarök. Snorri gives different names for these wolves but it is possible that he intentionally created the different identities or else they represent much later views imposed on what would be an older paradigm (Simek, 1993).

Hel

A child of Loki and a female Jotun, sometimes described as monstrous with half her body living and half dead. There is debate about whether she existed in the pagan era or was created to personify the realm of Helheim, which itself shows a lot of later Christian rewriting from a place of welcome and rest to one synonymous with the Christian Hell as a place of suffering. According to the Prose Edda when the Aesir took Loki's children from Jotunheim, Odin sent Hel to Helheim[38] and he:

> ...gave to her power over nine worlds, to apportion all abodes among those that were sent to her: that is, men dead of sickness or of old age. She has great possessions there; her walls are exceeding high and her gates great.

Jorð

Jorð's name means earth and she is an eponymous earth goddess who is considered both one of the Aesir as well as a female Jotun. Thor is her son, making her at the least one of Odin's paramours. Her mother is Nott (night) and her father is Anarr.

There are multiple goddesses whose names are various forms of the word for earth, but it's unclear if they are all Jorð under different names, all poetic references to one goddess, or individual beings (Simek, 1993).

Jormungandr

One of three monstrous children of Loki and the female Jotun, Angrboda, Jormungandr's name means 'huge monster' but in English he is most often called either the Midgard Serpent or World Serpent (Simek, 1993). Jormungandr is said to lay below the water and encircle the world; in one account Thor pulls him up while fishing, or at least raises his head, but he is freed before fully surfacing. During Ragnarök he will fight Thor who will kill him, but Jormungandr will poison Thor so that he dies within steps of their battle.

Mani

The god of the moon, as the Norse had a moon god and sun goddess. His name is the word for moon and according to the Prose Edda the gods were so offended that his father named him this, and named his sister sun, in praise of their beauty that they took the children and set them up carrying light through the sky. As Snorri describes it: *"Mani steers the course of the moon, and determines its waxing and waning."*. The Voluspa doesn't offer such a detailed backstory but it does claim that the Gods set up Mani in order to keep track of time during the year. This likely reflects the older way of measuring periods of time and the timing of events by the moon's cycle (Simek, 1993). At Ragnarök he will be caught and consumed by the wolf that chases him through the sky.

Mímir

Counted among the Jotun but also listed as one of the Aesir, Mímir is Odin's uncle and is sent to the Vanir as a peace hostage. Mímir possesses the Well of Mímir which is a source of wisdom as is Mímir himself, either through his own knowledge or through drinking from the well.

Mímir is sent to the Vanir as a peace hostage but is beheaded by them after it is found out that he is secretly advising the other hostage, Hoenur, so that he seems much wiser than he is. Receiving Mímir's head back from the Vanir, Odin preserves it with herbs and spells so that it continues to advise him. When Ragnarök begins it is to Mímir's head that Odin goes for counsel.

Nerthus

A Germanic deity who some scholars link to the Norse Njorð, although that is purely speculative[39]. Viewed as an earth goddess. Tacitus in Germania relates a story about Nerthus having a shrine on an island where a statue of her is kept. This statue is taken out and carried around in a cart pulled by cattle, tended to by a priest, and when it is returned to the shrine it is first washed and the slaves who washed it were then ritually drowned.

Rán

A female Jotun, Rán is strongly associated with the sea and particularly with drowned sailors. It is said that those who drown are caught in Rán's nets and taken to an afterlife in her realm at the bottom of the sea. Idioms related to drowning, such as the one just mentioned, refer to Rán and she is seen as having dominion over the realm of the sea-dead.

Her name may be related to the word for robber (Simek, 1993). This is likely an illusion to her taking sailors into her realm. She is the wife of Aegir and probably the mother of his nine daughters. Simek suggests that as Aegir was the welcoming, helpful ocean, Rán was the deadly side of it.

Sunna

Also known as Sól, she is the eponymous goddess of the sun and sister to Mani, god of the moon. They are the children of a man named Mundilfari whose praise of their beauty caused the Aesir to take them and place them in the sky, assigning them their duties. As Snorri describes it:

*they caused Sunna to drive those horses that drew the chariot of the
sun, which the gods had fashioned, for the world's illumination,
from that glowing stuff which flew out of Muspelheim.*

Sunna's exact nature is unclear although in the Gylfaginning she
is called 'elfin beam' indicating that she may be of the Álfar. At
Ragnarök she will be consumed by a giant wolf and afterwards
her daughter will take her place in the sky.

Chapter 9

Other Spirits

The Gods, by any name, are not the only beings found in Norse belief and no book on the pantheon would be complete if we didn't also discuss these related spirits. Often there is a very fine line between the Gods and some of these other spirits who seem to occupy a blurry space between humans and deities or may even be included among the deities in some cases. There is often confusion between the different types as well, particularly Álfar and Dvergar, and Álfar and human dead. So, while this chapter is meant to offer a selection of other spirits that are important in Norse spirituality and are connected to the Norse pantheon in various ways, it should be understood that none of these are truly hard and fast categories and there is inevitably interplay between them.

Álfar

The word Álfar is most often given in English as elves and often more widely understood through that lens. However, one of the challenges in understanding the Norse and Germanic material is that many different Otherworldly beings may be called Álfar or have names involving the word Álfar. The Norse word Álfar appears in German as Alp or Elb, and English as Elf, while in modern Icelandic they are known as both Álfar and Huldufolk (hidden folk), although Huldufolk is also used as a generic term, like elf, that can describe Álfar, trolls and land spirits. Land wights are also sometimes conflated with the Álfar, because the two have many commonalities, but also key differences that indicate they actually are separate types of beings (Gundarsson, 2007). The modern view of elves as tiny laborers is vastly at odds with the traditional view of the Álfar as tall, beautiful, and powerful beings. If you are familiar with Tolkien's elves then you have some idea of the older view of the Álfar.

The Álfar were created when the Gods created the world and in Norse myth one of the nine worlds belongs to them: Ljossalfheim (Light Elf Home). Properly there are at least three groups referred to as Álfar in Norse myth: the Ljósálfar (light elves), Svartálfar (literally black elves; often conflated with Dvergar - dwarves), and Dökkálfar (literally dark elves; mound dead) although it is difficult to know with certainty if these were originally seen as different beings altogether which were all later simply called Álfar for convenience, or if they were always seen as related beings. Jacob Grimm tried, in his Teutonic Mythology, to make a literal division of the groups by color, so that the Ljósálfar were white, the Svartálfar black and the Dökkálfar grey, but this is almost certainly his own invention (Grimm, 1883). I think it is more likely, personally, that Álfar was sometimes used as a term to describe supernatural beings who were neither Gods nor Jotuns and so could be used in a more general sense, as well as specifically with the Ljósálfar probably being the original beings under that name. In the lore, however, we do see beings referred to as Álfar at one point and elsewhere as other types of beings, including gods or Jotuns, so it can be difficult to have any real clarity on this. There is some clear distinction between the Ljósálfar, the more traditionally understood Otherworldly elves, and the Dökkálfar, who are understood to be the mound-dead, but there is also significant crossover as well which may indicate an understood connection between the two groups (Gundarsson, 2007).

Discussing the Álfar is complicated because they appear in mythology as both one cohesive grouping and subdivided into more specific groupings, as discussed above. Often in Norse myth we simply see references to the Álfar, often paired with but distinct from the Aesir, giving us phrases like in the Voluspo *"How fare the Aesir? How fare the Álfar?"* and this one from the

Lokasenna *"From the Gods and elves who are gathered here..."*[40]. Yet we also find distinct groups mentioned among the Álfar that seem to have their own characteristics and descriptors, the Ljósálfar, Dökkálfar, and Svartálfar. It is possible that these distinct groups are literary conventions, created later to better define different mythic motifs, or to reflect foreign influences. Certainly in modern times we see only the general grouping of Álfar in folklore and the word álf is used in compounds such as land-elf and waterfall-elf, implying that álf has more general connotations.

In the Prose Edda we see Snorri mentioning distinct types of Álfar who appear in mythology, the Ljósálfar and the Svartálfar. A third group of Álfar, the Dökkálfar also appear in mythology.

- *Ljósálfar* - their name means 'light elves' and they live in a world called Alfheim [elf home] or Ljósálfheim [light elf home] that according to mythology belongs to the Vanic deity Freyr. The connection to Freyr has led to some speculation about a deeper connection between them and the Vanir. The Ljósálfar are described by Snorri as being beautiful and fair to see. Ljósálfar are said to influence the weather and like the Aesir, Dvergar, Humans, and Jotuns they possess runes given to them by Odin.
- *Dökkálfar* - The Dökkálfar are referenced in a few places in Norse mythology. The name itself means 'dark elves' and Snorri describes them as living in the earth. Grimm calls them *'Genii obscuri'* or spirits of the dark and suggests a connection between them and nâir, spirits of the dead, even going so far as to place them living *"in hel, the heathen hades"* (Grimm, 1888, p446). Grimm also questions whether the Dökkálfar should be separated from the nâir or whether *"[t]he dusky elves are souls of dead men..."* (Grimm, 1888, p 447). There is some strong evidence that the Dökkálfar were the mound dead or male ancestors

and the Dökkálfar are sometimes called Mound Elves; it is not certain, however, and it may be that some Dökkálfar are human dead but others are not[41].

- *Svartálfar* - meaning 'black elves' they possess their own world, Svartálfheim [black elf home]. The Duergar or dwarves also live in Svartálfheim creating a longstanding confusion about whether Svartálfar are truly elves in their own right or are actually another name for dwarves. Both are associated with mountains and mountainous regions, but seem to have a distinct and separate focus in activities and interactions with people. Grimm believes that the Svartálfar were good natured beings and argues that they received worship from people into the 19th century.

The Álfar are a complicated and fascinating group in mythology and we have barely touched on them here. Consider this merely a brief introduction to some basic ideas about the Álfar as they appear in Norse mythology but bear in mind that they can be found throughout Germanic/Norse folklore. They are beings that are both benevolent and dangerous as the mood suits and depending on how they are treated, like the elves found across folklore.

The Álfar are known to interbreed with the other beings, particularly humans, and some mythic heroes and kings (as well as the king's half-sister in the Saga of King Hrolf Kraki) were said to be half-elven. Icelandic patronyms sometimes show this possible ancestral connection (Gundarsson, 2007). This may reflect the common belief that the birthrate among the elves is low or that females are rare; a common theme in mythology is the stealing of brides and babies or of midwives to help at births. In the older Norse material Álfar always appear to be male, although in later Icelandic folklore we see females as well, and in the Swedish material we mainly see álf women (Gundarsson, 2007).

Álfar are associated with their own world, Ljossalfheim, of course, but are also believed to live in or access our world through natural sites including mountains, cliffs, and boulders. They are known to be associated with certain places, and particularly certain individual trees, and it is believed that to disturb the places belonging to the Hidden Folk is very bad luck (Gundarsson, 2007). As recently as October 2013 protesters in Iceland were trying to block a highway project on the grounds that the construction passed through an area belonging to the Álfar, who would be angered (Scherker, 2013). It is believed by many that disturbing the Álfar with construction will result in bad luck and machines breaking down and often a special person who is known to be able to see and communicate with the elves will be brought in to negotiate (Gruber, 2007). Those who are brave enough to enter an álf-hill or visit the realm of the Álfar may find that time moves very differently there, and sometimes the Álfar will not release those who have gone among them.

In folklore the Álfar are seen as being especially active during the twelve days of Yule and at Midsummer. Gundarsson suggests - and I have long agreed - that the summer activities of the Álfar, while still potentially perilous to humans, are less dangerous in nature and intent than the Yule activities (Gundarsson, 2007). The Álfar ride out in full procession at midsummer and Yule, an activity which may convey blessing on the areas they pass through, but in Iceland the Yule ride of the Álfar, the alfarieth, is equated to the Wild Hunt and is extremely dangerous to see or contact (Gundarsson, 2007).

Interacting with the Álfar is always a tricky business, as they can give blessings or lay curses on a person. In many traditional tales those who encounter elves and please them - often with good manners and generosity - may receive gifts, but those who offend them are killed or driven mad. When offered a gift from the Álfar one should not refuse, and these gifts might include food, drink, or worthless things like leaves which will later turn to gold (Gundarsson, 2007). The Álfar can also heal illnesses and injuries, if properly petitioned, and can be called on with a specific ceremony to protect a baby (Gundarsson, 2007).

The Álfar are angered by several types of human activity including the aforementioned disturbance of their places. They are also driven out of an area by the placing of an alfreka or by people urinating on the ground (Pennick, 1993; Gundarsson, 2007). When angered they can cause bad luck, sickness, madness, or death. Elves were also thought to be able to inflict illness on humans through the use of alf-shot or an elf-blast, the first being a small, invisible arrow that created diseases including bone cancer and arthritis, the second being a method where the elves would breathe or blow sickness into a person. There are several surviving charms aimed at curing alfshot (Gundarsson, 2007). There is also a reference in older material to "alf-seidhr" possibly a type of magic worked by the Álfar against humans to cause madness and death[42] (Gundarsson, 2007). It is equally possible, as Heath discusses in 'Elves, Witches & Gods', that alf-seidhr was a cooperative practice between Álfar and witches which would be supported by material found across Anglo-Saxon sources.

In Norse lore iron and steel are used as a protection against dangerous Álfar and other spirits, although it is not effective against Jotuns (Gundarsson, 2007). Any item made of this metal may be used, but traditionally bladed weapons and nails were the most commonly seen, and iron or steel nails might be hammered into a post or doorway to protect a home. Sulfur, rowan, and juniper are also traditional Norse protections, as well as a blend of woody nightshade, orchid and tree sap which was said to protect against the "unwanted attentions" of the huldufolk (Gundarsson, 2007). It is also said that church bells ringing will drive off the Álfar, as will Christian prayers, although this may perhaps represent more of a reaction by the Álfar to a religion which offends them than a sign of any power that faith actually has over them.

It is wise to remember to honor the Álfar, with rituals and offerings. The Álfar are closer to us and our world and affect us more often than the Gods generally do, and they should be respected. It is also a good idea to understand how the Álfar can affect us, for good and ill, and ways to best deal with them.

A specific place associated with the Álfar are the álfur steinn, or elf-stone. Elf-stones, called elf-stenar in Swedish, are boulders with cup like indentations, or that are strongly associated as being the homes of the Álfar, and are believed to have healing powers (Lockey, 1882; Towrie, 2013). These boulders were places that people would go to make vows, and to leave offerings which ranged from lard and butter to copper coins, flowers, and ribbons (Lockey, 1882).

Ancestors

Ancestors can form a key aspect of Heathen practice and belief, both those who are ancestors by blood and those who are ancestors in other ways, such as through marriage, adoption, or fellowship. In modern belief there are also many people who support the idea of ancestors of skill or affinity, that is people with no direct relationship who are connected through a similar job, career, or interest. How strictly or fluidly ancestors are understood will depend on the individual or the tradition but I prefer to take a broad view.

Ancestors can and do continue to watch over and interact with us. This is not in any way a new belief but is one we find across historic Heathenry as well. Sometimes protective ancestors were given other names such as the Dísir who are female guardians of the family line, or the Álfar which may include male ancestors. Ancestors were significant enough to the pre-Christian Heathens that we have accounts of Heathens who refused conversion to Christianity out of fear it would mean being cut off from their ancestors and being denied a place with them after death.

The core belief behind including ancestors in our spiritual practice is that they are the most motivated to care about our welfare and most willing to aid us when they can in our lives. Remembering ancestors and continuing to speak of their memory also keeps them empowered and in existence.

Dísir

Also called Idises, a dís is a kind of protective female spirit. In Norse literature the Dísir appear to be a kind of fetch[43] spirit that shows up in dreams (Simek, 1993). Another view sees the Dísir as dead human women, specifically ancestors who are tied to their family line and watch over their descendants. This is complicated because the word itself is used to mean everything from women to, possibly, a type of goddess, so that all that's clear is that it indicates someone female (Simek, 1993).

There was a holiday celebrated for the Dísir called a Dísirblót. The dating is uncertain with one source claiming mid-October while the other simply mentions February; it is also unclear what the celebration would have involved beyond a feast (Simek, 1993).

Draugar

Draugar are a kind of undead human found in Norse myth and folklore. They are sometimes falsely equated to zombies or ghosts but this is inaccurate as draugar are a different type of being. They represent the living dead, or spirits who remain within their own corpse after death, and often continue trying to interact with the living. They are tangible and physical creatures that are capable of speech, moving things, and harming living humans. Simek suggest the term may have originally meant 'harmful spirit', and they are certainly viewed as harmful and dangerous beings that must be destroyed. Like the vampire of eastern European folk belief, to kill a draugar one must decapitate it and then burn it before burying the ashes in some wild area (Simek, 1993).

Dvergar

Dvergar, Anglicized as dwarves, survived in folklore fairly intact after Christianization as they were separate from religion and viewed differently than the Aesir or even the Álfar (Simek, 1993). Because of this there is more material on dwarves than we may have on other types of beings and the material is probably closer to the older beliefs than we find with beings who were later heavily Christianized. Unlike the later understanding of them, Dvergar were not originally seen as small or short, but were envisioned as tall beings; the description of Dvergar as small and ugly was a later development (Simek, 1993). The most notable features of Dvergar across the source material is their wisdom and skill, particularly skill at crafting. It is the Dvergar who created the treasures of the Aesir, including Thor's hammer, Mjolnir, and who first brewed the mead of poetry. In the Prose Edda we learn that four Dvergar hold up the four corners of the sky in each of the cardinal directions and various sources describe the dwarves being created or originating from the corpse of the primordial Jotun, Ymir.

The Álfar and the Dvegar - elves and dwarves – can be difficult groups to entirely sort out. On one hand there are some good arguments that the two may actually be the same, with Svartálfar and potentially Dökkálfar both simply being alternate names for Dvergar. This is supported by three main things: many Dvergar have names that incorporate the word álf' such as Vindalf and Gandalf[44]; the Svartálfar were said to live in Svartálfheim but the Dvergar live there as well; and the svartálfar and Dökkálfar were said to live beneath the ground or in mounds. However, there is also evidence that might support the argument that the two groups were separate, including that they are occasionally referenced in the same work together as different groups. In verse 25 of Hrafnagaldr Óðins we see the Dökkálfar being grouped together with Jotuns, dead men, and dwarves: *"gýgjur og þursar, náir, Dvergar og dökkálfar"* [Female Jotuns and Thurses[45], dead men, dwarves and dark elves]. This would at the least seem to indicate some degree of separation between Dvergar and Dökkálfar. In the Alvissmál it is also established that the Álfar and Dvergar have different languages and kennings for things, which would also indicate separation of the two groups (Gundarsson, 2007). For the most part the Álfar would seem to be beings closely tied to the Gods, perhaps one step beneath them in power and influence, beings who can influence weather and possess powerful magic that can affect people's health. The Dvergar are associated with mining and smithcraft and are not as closely tied to the Gods; when they appear in myth dealing with the Gods they must always be negotiated with or otherwise dealt with in some fashion diplomatically.

Einherjar

The word einherjar means 'those who fight alone' and is the special term used for the warriors killed in battle who go to Valhalla (Simek, 1993). They spend their days in Valhalla fighting each other to the death but are all alive again at night and go in to Odin's hall to feast and celebrate. They drink mead which comes from the goat Heidrun and eat meat prepared from the pig Saehrimnir, which is killed and revived even as they are every day.

The key role of the Einherjar is to fight against the Jotuns on the side of the Aesir during Ragnarök. Although they have been rather heavily romanticized in recent years the Einherjar are a very specific type of being who are gathered and exist entirely to defend Asgard as elite warriors.

Jotuns

Jotuns, often translated as giants, usually have a negative reputation but the truth is more nuanced. There are Jotuns who aid the Aesir and are allied with them and there are Jotuns that are entirely antithetical to both the Aesir and humanity. They live in a world, Jotunheim, which is described as being cold, fierce, and dangerous and presents challenges to those who travel in it.

While the Dvergar and Álfar were created by the Aesir, the Jotuns came from the primordial being, Ymir, before the worlds were made. They are also very intertwined with the Aesir, being both sometimes counted among them, such as Gerd and Skadhi, or being the parents or one parent of a member of the Aesir. This intertwining reflects the convoluted connection between the two groups, where the Jotuns act as the main antagonists but also often the main allies of the Aesir. Some of this dichotomy in how Jotuns were perceived is seen in the two main old Norse terms for them, Jotunn and þurs, where Jotunn was a neutral term and þurs indicated the more dangerous types (Simek, 1993).

House Spirits

Folklore is full of beings that fall under the broad category of house spirits. These might be types of fairies, or spirits-of-place, or spirits connected to particular families living in a location. What makes them house spirits is simply their association with human habitations; some of them prefer to shelter in human homes, some of them like attaching themselves to humans, and some simply exist in human built structures. Most house spirits seem to enjoy being around humans, although that can vary widely depending on the humans. Some will follow a family even if they move while others are stationary and will remain in the same location over time. If the subject interests you I suggest Claude Lecouteux's book 'The Tradition of Household Spirits' to dig deeper into the topic.

There are several specific types of house spirits in various cultures that each have different folklore and therefore ways to be understood and related to. The main two we are looking at here come from Scandinavian and German folklore.

- Nisse/Tomte – the Danish or Norwegian term for a house spirit is Nisse while in Sweden or Finland they are called Tomte. The Nisse or Tomte appear as a small, bearded man who helps with chores around a house or farm. As long as they are treated respectfully, they are protective spirits but if offended they can turn malicious. It is traditional around the winter solstice or Christmas eve in modern Scandinavian countries to offer a bowl of sweetened porridge to the Nisse; this porridge must have a large pat of butter on top (not stirred in) to show respect for the Nisse's hard work through the year.

- Kobolds – in Germany we find house spirits being referred to as kobolds[46], which were thought to protect and clean a home, either being attached to a specific family or building. These particular house spirits were sometimes represented by dolls or similar objects, but there may have been prohibitions against drawing images of them (Lecouteux, 2000). Like other house spirits they were thought to be helpful unless offended in which case they could become troublesome.

Land Spirits

Land spirits, like house spirits, are a diverse collection of beings that we tend to categorize as land spirits to make discussing them easier. They may be called landvaettir or land wights in Norse practice. Individual land spirits may be better understood under other specific terms, perhaps nature spirits or spirits-of-place. Scholars do not agree on the exact nature or history of land spirits, with some suggesting they are the human dead while others see them as a kind of nature spirit. Ellis Davidson argues for the nature spirit theory because there is evidence in the Icelandic Sagas of humans encountering land spirits where no humans had previously lived or died (Ellis Davidson, 1988). Generally the best way I can define a land spirit is that it is a spirit tied to a specific location or natural feature, as they are usually associated with a very specific place or geographic feature, such as a boulder or waterfall. Land spirits are protective beings who guard the areas that belong to them and can also influence that place to either succeed or fail. Lecouteux has a book, 'Demons and Spirits of the Land', that can be useful here, although I'd also suggest looking around at other sources of material on land spirits such as the anthology 'Spirits of Place' edited by Reppion.

Land spirits are seen as essential to the protection of a space and also of its prosperity. In Egil's Saga, the eponymous main character curses the king and queen of Norway by raising a niðstang which offends and drives away the land spirits. Similarly it is said that when Viking longships came into ports or travelled up rivers in Iceland they had to take the dragon head off the front of their ship lest it offend the land spirits.

Iceland is strongly connected to its land spirits, so much so that the four main ones are depicted on the coat of arms of the country and its coins. There is a story which tells of a magician who came to Iceland in the form of a whale to do harm there and found it full of land spirits and guarded by four great spirits. Approaching from the east he was confronted by a land spirit in the form of a great dragon. Swimming northward he found an enormous eagle. In the west there was a huge bull, and in the south a protective Jotun. Eventually the magician had to give up and leave as the island was too well protected by its land spirits.

Matronae

The Matronae, whose name simply means "Mothers" in Latin, are found in Gaulish, Roman, and Germanic sources (Lendering, 2013). These goddesses are known from over 80 inscriptions on images found from France to Germany and through northern Italy, and can be found on hundreds of votive altars (Evans, 2005). The Matronae are usually depicted as three seated women holding symbols of abundance, including fruit, animals, infants, and cornucopias, as well as items like small pieces of cloth, basins, and spindles; the women wear long skirts and have one breast bare, possibly symbolizing a nursing mother (Evans, 2005; Green, 1992). Often the figures on the sides are shown wearing wide hats and sitting next to trees while the central figure has loose hair; in one case the inscription was accompanied by an image of a tree, a snake, and a goat (Lendering, 2013; Green, 1992). Images also depict the Matronae being worshiped by women and by soldiers and being offered fruit and bread (Green, 1992). Although it's difficult to know with certainty what the Matronae were worshiped for, most scholars surmise that they were related to fertility, abundance, healing, and protection. Many Matronae had distinctive names relating to the area they were in or people who worshiped them so it is also possible that they represented communal maternal ancestors, an idea supported by inscriptions naming them "matres paternae" which may be translated as ancestral mothers (Lendering, 2013). It is also possible that the Matronae were examples of cults of genii loci [spirits of place] expressed in a set form, although Ross suggests that they are reflexes of tribal mother goddesses (Green, 1992; Ross, 1998). In specific locations the Matronae also had specific associations: the Matres Comedovae and the Matres Griselicae were associated with healing and specific healing springs, for example (Green, 1992).

Norns

The Norns are complex figures in Norse mythology, appearing as both a group of three specific deities as well as a more general type of being. We will start by looking at the specific Norns and then discuss the more general type of spirit under that name. They are described this way in the Poetic Edda:

Thence come the maidens mighty in wisdom,
Three from the dwelling down 'neath the tree;

Urth is one named, Verthandi the next,–
On the wood they scored,– and Skuld the third.
Laws they made there, and life allotted
To the sons of men, and set their fates.

Urð is the first Norn mentioned of the three. Her name means 'fate' and the word for it is connected more widely to the word for wyrd. Her name is also connected to both the word for 'became' and also the well of Urð, one of the three primal wells of Norse mythology and the one in which the fate of all is created (Simek, 1993). She was seen as the being responsible for the past and that which has already been done. The second Norn is Verðandi, who is connected to that which is happening in the ever-moving present moment. Her name is related to the word for 'becoming' (Simek, 1993). The final Norn of the three is Skuld, who is associated with the future or that which hasn't happened yet. Simek suggests her name may mean either blame or future, although it's uncertain. The three together are seen as the embodiment and arbiters of fate from a Norse point of view, tending the well from which all fates come and into which all actions go. As embodiments of such a primal force they are also generally viewed as neutral parties who don't choose a person's destiny so much as shape it from the raw material the person themselves creates through a complex web of their family's previous actions, their own choices, and their reactions to events.

Besides the three fate-setting Norns who tend the well of Urd, we also find a variety of other norns who may perhaps be viewed as lesser spirits although they are still powerful and influential on a person's life. These are less of a cohesive type of being so much as a job description, in that there are norns who are Aesir, elves, and dwarves, and one might suggest human ancestors as well although that is based more on later adaptations in folklore than mythology.

> ...*there are many norns: those who come to each child that is born,
> to appoint his life; these are of the race of the gods, but the second
> are of the Elf-people, and the third are of the kindred of the dwarves,
> as it is said here:*
> *Most sundered in birth I say the Norns are;*
> *They claim no common kin:*
> *Some are of Æsir-kin, some are of Elf-kind,*
> *Some are Dvalinn's daughters.*[47]

The Prose Edda acknowledges that the norns do not give out
luck fairly but rather that some have exceedingly good luck and
others very difficult lives. This is explained with the idea that
there are both 'good' norns and 'evil' norns who can affect a
person: "*Good norns and of honorable race appoint good life; but those
men that suffer evil fortunes are governed by evil norns.*" (Brodeur,
1916). Unlike the three Norns these other norns do directly
influence a person's life by effecting their luck, hence the idea
of good and evil norns, that is those who help a person succeed
and those who cause a person difficulty. Norns can be helpful
in childbirth or in healing work but may also cause difficulties,
placing them in a powerful but nebulous category that may
overlap with Valkyries, Dísir, and matronae (Simek, 1993).

Trolls

The word means monster or giant and was used interchangeably
for Jotuns, particularly the more dangerous or malevolent kinds
(Simek, 1993). Over time, however, the word came to have its
own distinct meaning so that trolls and Jotuns were understood
as separate types of beings, although they were both similarly
large and ugly in later folklore. They were sometimes confused
with Draugar, and were known to live in caves (Simek, 1993).
In modern folklore trolls have a a more magical quality to them
and are known to steal humans as well as to switch their own
babies for human babies, similar to the folklore of Celtic fairies.

Valkyries

The word Valkyrie means 'choosers of the slain' and that accurately describes who and what they are. Closely associated with Odin the Valkyries are female spirits who serve him by gathering those killed in battle to bring them to Valhalla. They seemed to have existed earlier as a more primal force but later took on their strong association with Odin, being called both Oðins meyar [Odin's girls] and Oskmeyar [wish girls] as they were seen to represent enactors of Odin's will (Simek, 1993). In the lists of Valkyries that we have they are usually numbered at 9 or 12 or 13 but there doesn't seem to have ever been either a set number nor a specific named grouping.

In the existing myths the Valkyries act to choose the slain and determine who wins in conflicts, at Odin's will, and also bring the chosen to Valhalla. In Valhalla some of them serve drinks to the heroes.

The most well-known Valkyrie may be Sigdrifa, who falls in love with a human hero. Brynhildr of Wanger's opera is another famous Valkyrie.

The Wild Hunt

The Wild Hunt is a collection of spirits – what type varies by the exact folklore – that travel through the air in storms led by a Huntsman. Who the Huntsman is varies as widely as the geographic areas the hunt is found in and the names it is known by, but often it features a deity as the Huntsman or Huntswoman. The Wild Hunt is found in Germany, France, Denmark, Normandy, Sweden, Norway, England, Scotland, Ireland, Wales, and the United States (Jones, 2003). The Hunt is interesting though in that although found across a wide geographic area and among different cultures it always takes on a unique local character, often with a specific local spirit or God taking on the role of Huntsman, so that while the wider concept is cohesive the individual folklore can be very different.

In the Germanic areas the Hunt is often led by Odin under the name Wodan, Frau Hulde, or both together, while in other places the leader may be a god, ghost, or famous historic figure (Jones, 2003). The hunt in Germany is also sometimes led by Frau Perchta or the White Lady, Frau Gode[48], who led groups of dead children or witches through the sky and were seen as good omens of abundant crops in the coming year (Berk, & Spytma, 2002). Some modern sources try to relate the Hunt in France led by Harlequin to the Norse goddess Hel, but it more likely that the name derives from the 12th century term "Herlethingus", a word used to describe wandering spectral troops during the time of Henry II (Berk, & Spytma, 2002). In Orkney the Hunt is led by Odin but may also be the trows[49] riding out on pale horses to steal cows (Towrie, 2013). Often when the Huntsman - or woman - is not a God or Otherworldly spirit it is said to be a person who so loved hunting in life that they rejected any other afterlife but to continue hunting and were rewarded or cursed to perpetually hunt for all eternity (Grimm, 1883).

The Wild Hunt is known by many names. In Orkney it is called the Raging Host (Towrie, 2013). Associated with Odin the Hunt was called Odin's Hunt [Odensjakt], Odin's Army, the Wild Ride [Wilde Jagd], Asgardeia, Oskerei, Oensjagearen [Odin's Hunters], Odens Jakt [Odin's Hunt], Horrific Ride, Thunderous Ride, and also the Ride of the Dead, and the Family of Harlequin (in France) (Towrie, 2013; Berk, & Spytma, 2002). Other names include the Furious Host or Wild Host and in America, the Ghost Riders.

The Wild Hunt travels in the air, and appears as a group of dark riders, led by a Huntsmen who may be headless, with a pack of fearsome hounds, and accompanied by a horde of spirits who sometimes appear as the newly dead or battle dead (Jones, 2003). The Hunt always includes horses and hounds, both usually black, but sometimes white or grey, and always fierce; in some accounts the animals' breath fire and they are often missing limbs or with extra limbs and may display the same gruesome wounds as the battle dead accompanying the Hunt (Berk, & Spytma, 2002). The presence of the Hunt is signaled by the unearthly sound of hooves, hunting horns, and baying hounds appearing usually in the night sky and sometimes in storms (Towrie, 2013).

Mary Jones gives us a classic description of the Hunt from 1127 CE:

> ...it was seen and heard by many men: many hunters riding. The hunters were black, and great and loathy, and their hounds all black, and wide-eyed and loathy, and they rode on black horses and black he-goats. This was seen in the very deer park in the town of Peterborough, and in all the woods from the same town to Stamford; and the monks heard the horn blowing that they blew that night. Truthful men who kept watch at night said that it seemed to them that there might be about twenty or thirty horn blowers. This was seen and heard...all through Lenten tide until Easter. (Jones, 2003)

This description gives the time the Hunt appears as during Lent which might be assumed to be roughly March and April. In Switzerland the Hunt was said to appear during summer nights, and those who do not quickly get out of the way of the passing Hunt will be trampled by it (Grimm, 1883). More often in folklore the Hunt was said to ride in late fall and winter, particularly during the 12 nights of Yule. Grimm tells us that in Germany it was believed the Hunt rode during the time from Christmas to 12th Night or whenever the storm winds blew (Grimm, 1883). Yule was seen as a time of high supernatural influence when the dead were more present (Towrie, 2013). In my own experience with the Ghost Riders of America they appear around Samhain and ride until the first week of January, but in times of great unrest or disturbance they may appear as well.

In many cases the Hunt is connected to the spirits of the dead;

Towrie conjectures that the Orkney trows, themselves connected to the Wild Hunt, may have originally been considered spirits of the dead (Towrie, 2013). The dead are often seen in the retinue of the Hunt and that includes both those who may be recognized as recently dead as well as the ancient battle dead, some displaying hideous wounds. Some folklore also says that the wild Hunt rides out seeking the dead, chasing certain types of ghosts or spirits.

The Hunt appeared for different reasons depending on where it was - in some cases hunting a mythic animal or creature, in others pursuing lost souls or even seeking to punish wrong-doers (Towrie, 2013). In some cases the Hunt might offer to take a living person to ride with them, but the risk of doing so was great; the person might never return or might become a permanent part of the Host. Seeing the Hunt could be an ill-omen and the Hunt itself could kill or drive a person mad, but conversely in some areas it was believed meeting the Hunt bravely and politely could earn a person great reward. There are several folk tales, like the story of *"Wod, the Wild Huntsman"* where the main character meets the Hunt and comes away with gifts of meat and gold as a reward for his cleverness. Showing proper respect would also earn a person a reward, but conversely rudeness would result in the person being thrown a severed human limb, if he was lucky, or his own dead child, if he wasn't; in some cases the Hunt would turn on the person mocking them and tear the person to pieces (Berk, & Spytma, 2002; Grimm, 1883).

Protection from the Wild Hunt is best achieved through avoiding them by not traveling at night, especially during Yule or other dangerous times. Shelter can also be sought at the first sound of hunting horn or hounds in the air. However, should those fail or not be possible and should you meet the Hunt, and do not feel like taking your chances with them, there is this charm from 14th century Germany:

Woden's host and all his men
Who are bearing wheels and willow twigs
Broken on the wheel and hanged.
You must go away from here.
(Gundarsson, trans. Höfler; Berk, & Spytma, 2002)

The folklore of the Wild Hunt is certainly very old and Kershaw in 'Odin, The One Eyed God' suggests that it may have originated with a cult of Odin that involved masked figures, which later evolved into beliefs about, or was always connected to, the idea of Odin's role as leader of a portion of the dead.

Conclusion

The Norse Pantheon, and indeed Norse belief, is a complex and wide-ranging thing which encompasses several distinct cultures across many centuries. Each of these cultures had and has its own approach to belief and practice that can be seen in mythology and folklore. And yet we find a distinct thread running throughout it all which gives it some cohesion into the modern day. Those seeking to follow the faith of the Aesir (or the pantheon by any name) have a great deal of material to work with and a large corpus of myths and folklore to draw from, which have only been skimmed here; I strongly encourage those interested in learning more to continue this journey by seeking out the Lore for themselves. I have heard it said that Asatru is the religion with homework and I find that to be true. One way or another this is a spirituality that challenges a person to keep learning and keep searching, no matter how long one has been in the community.

There is a beauty in the old stories, the Lore, and besides teaching us of the Gods and spirits they also speak to struggles that are very human and very tangible. We read about the beings we worship dealing with things that humans also deal with, from grief to love to anger. These are relatable beings and not only can we understand the struggles and motivations of the Aesir but we it is logical to believe that they too can understand the joys and pains of our lives. These are not beings that have no experience with loss, success, and concern and that makes them much more relatable. Which isn't to anthropomorphize them too much – they are still Gods and beyond our full ability to comprehend – but there is a comfort in knowing that they too celebrate marriages and have funerals and must work to keep their security. Life is not easy for humans, but the Lore shows us that it is not necessarily easy for the Aesir either within their own context.

In this book we have discussed the broad strokes of Heathen belief and have looked at the Gods and spirits (by many names) that enrich those beliefs and provide a foundation for spirituality and practice. Every person will relate to this material differently and will find a path forward from here in their own way, but ultimately, we are all working from the same sources and all seeking connection to the same Powers. Even the most diverse of approaches to the Norse pantheon shares more common ground than many people may like to admit.

We live in a world that is full of not only humans but trolls and Álfar, land spirits and Dísir, Dvergar and ancestors. All of this exists around us, whether we see it or not, just as the Aesir, Vanir, and other Powers exist around us whether we acknowledge them or not. But our lives can become so much richer if we choose reciprocity with these beings instead of ignoring them.

Where you go from here is up to you.

Appendix A – Terms

Like most spiritual traditions Heathenry, by any name, has specific terminology that is used within its communities. I'm going to include a brief selection of some of these terms here, including both names of specific approaches or groups as well as terms for particular things. These are simplified descriptions to give the reader the basics of the concepts, not in-depth descriptions.

Álfatru – literally 'belief in elves', a term used both simply for people who believe the Álfar exist as well as sometimes by people who focus their spirituality on them.

Asatru – 'belief in the Aesir', the Icelandic term used for people who worship the Aesir. A follower of such a practice would be called Asatruar.

Blót – originally used for sacrificial rituals to the gods, blót means blood. However, in modern usage it can refer to any ritual honouring the gods and including an offering to them.

Einherjar – epic heroes gathered at death by the Valkyrie and living in Odin's hall in Asgard.

Faining – a simple ritual where various things like mead may be offered to the gods or other spirits.

Frith – an old English word meaning peace or security.

Galdr – spoken or chanted runes.

Germanic Paganism – Heathenry which focuses specifically on German Gods, spirits, and beliefs.

Godhi – term for a priest.

Grith – an old English concept of legal peace or security. In heathenry it is often used to describe the behaviour that is expected at events and gatherings.

Gythia – term for a priestess.

Heathenry – in this usage Heathenry refers to the beliefs and practices of people who follow pre-Christian Germanic/Norse Gods.

Innagard – literally inner yard, a concept in heathenry that can refer to people within a community.

Kindred – the name of a group of Heathens who practice together.

Norse Paganism – Heathenry which is specifically Norse focused.

Oath Ring – an oath ring is a large, usually arm band sized, ring that is used for swearing formal oaths.

Odinism – a term more commonly used by those inclined towards a racist version of Heathenry.

Ragnarök – the twilight or doom of the gods, Ragnarök is an event foretold by a seeress in which the Aesir will fight a final battle with the Jotuns and be destroyed.

Rokkatru – a term used by people who worship the Jotuns, including both the ones known to help the Aesir in myth and the ones antagonistic to them.

Seidhr – a type of historic magical practice that is referenced in the lore and has been reconstructed for modern use.

Seidhrkona – a woman who practices seidhr.

Spae – a term used for oracular or visionary practices.

Sumbel – a type of ritual where a horn is passed around a group and each person says something before drinking. The first round usually praises the gods, the second the ancestors, and the third (and beyond) can be used for personal boasts.

Theodism – Anglo-Saxon reconstructionism. Theodism is structured slightly differently from most other Heathen traditions and is usually more hierarchical.

Utgard – literally outer yard, a concept referring to those people or beings that are outside the bounds of a community.

Vanatru – a term used by people who focus specifically on the Vanic gods.

Vé – term for the altar used in Norse paganism, the word literally means 'shrine'.

Appendix B – Recommended Reading

I encourage people to look to the bibliography for suggestions of books but I'd also like to include a list of books that I'd reccomend people new to Heathenry read. These can be places to start and also offer a further or deeper look at specific topics.

1. Essential Asatru by Diana Paxson – a good introduction to the basics of belief and practice, particularly useful for those coming from a neopagan background.
2. A Practical Heathen's Guide to Asatru by Patricia Lafayllve – another solid intro book that will provide a different perspective from Paxson's.
3. The Way of Fire and Ice by Ryan Smith – one of the newer intros to Heathenry books on the market but one which has been very well received.
4. The Prose Edda – I suggest reading multiple translations to get the best understanding of the material.
5. The Poetic Edda – multiple translations are your friend.
6. Norse Myths by Kevin Crossley-Holland – Modern language retellings of the Eddic myths.
7. Norse Mythology by Neil Gaiman – another book of retellings of the myths, again it's good to get a couple perspectives here.
8. The Road to Hel by H.R. Ellis Davidson – an essential look at beliefs about the dead and afterlife. Generally speaking while a bit dated now but anything by this author is worth reading.
9. The Well and the Tree by Bauschatz – discusses cosmology from a heathen perspective.
10. 'Our Troth', volumes 1 and 2 – a very thorough look at everything from belief to practice, and a wonderful reference to have on hand.

11. Elves, Wights, and Trolls by K. Gundarsson – a look at the heathen belief in Otherworldly spirits, often not emphasized in American Heathenry but very important to understand.

12. Wights and Ancestors by Jenny Blain – a small book that digs into ideas around connecting to ancestors and spirits.

13. Elves, Witches, & Gods: Spinning Old Heathen Magic in the Modern Day by Cat Heath – an excellent dive into the more esoteric and experiential side of Heathenry.

14. Living Asatru by Greg Shelter – short but useful look at living modern Asatru.

15. We Are Our Deeds by Eric Wodening – a very in depth look at modern heathen ethics

16. Lady With a Mead Cup by Enright – a foundational work for constructing rituals.

If you are interested in specific deities I'd also suggest:

1. Freya, Lady, Vanadis by Patricia Lafayllve
2. Frey God of the World by Ann Groa Sheffield
3. Pagan Portals - Loki by Dagulf Loptson

I also have two books I have written on specific Norse gods: Pagan Portals - Odin and Pagan Portals - Thor

Endnotes

1. The people following these beliefs did not initially have any name for their own religion. The one in use today is that which was applied by outside cultures seeking to describe them.
2. It is outside the purview of this book to dig into this cultural influence but it should be considered, particularly in studying Icelandic beliefs around the Álfar which show striking similarities with Irish beliefs around the aos sidhe.
3. This is a very brief retelling of the general events. I highly recommend people read the full version of the Gylfaginning in the Prose Edda and Voluspa in the Poetic Edda to grasp the details.
4. This will be discussed in detail in the section on the afterlife in chapter 3.
5. Some groups outright ban calling Loki in their rituals, for example, while others welcome him as Odin's blood brother, and others find a middle ground by acknowledging him separately but not in the formal ritual.
6. Mead is the most common ritual offering, however, for people who do not or cannot drink alcohol there are many alternatives. This shouldn't be read in any way as implying that one must drink in order to be Heathen.
7. This practice was likely drawn from other forms of neopaganism and is not based in historical practices.
8. There are some exceptions to this, when giving what you have on hand is acceptable, but generally it's important to put in the effort to make an offering as valuable to you as possible.
9. Some choose to date it buy the first full moon of the year

instead. As with all things with Heathenry there are different approaches.

10. May 1st isn't Saint Walburga's saint's day but rather the day she was canonized in the Catholic church which is where it is theorized the name Walburgasnacht for that date comes from. According to Hodge's 'Waelburga and the Rites of May' it is also a day associated with healing miracles of saint Walburga. Several sources theorize that Walburga may be the name of an older pagan Goddess, particularly one named Walburga Frouwa, but it is difficult to prove.

11. It is worth noting that divorce was an option if the marriage went very badly.

12. I will note that perhaps unsurprisingly there was a notable double standard at play as to what behavior was expected from the man versus the woman in historic marriages, with chastity before marriage and fidelity during marriage expected of the woman while men often had lovers and mistresses. This is not a historic precedent that is carried forward in modern Heathen relationships, but is something you will find in researching the subject.

13. The boat burning burial may be slightly speculative although a few references are found to the practice but the idea is popular today, although often impractical.

14. All names used here are heiti or by-names of Odin.

15. Shamanism is a term for the beliefs and practices of specific cultural groups indigenous to northern Europe.

16. It's debated whether seidhr and spae were the same activities under different names or two different types of magical practices. For our purposes here we will be discussing them together.

17. Aelfe, the Anglo-Saxon term for Álfar or Elves.

18. The original Nine Noble Virtues were created in 1974 by founding members of the Odinic Rite who were also

members of the British Union of Fascists.

19. This is expanded from material previously published in my book Pagan Portals - Odin

20. Wight is a term found in Older English and Scots which means any sentient living being, somewhat analogous to 'spirit', used in modern Heathenry for a variety of beings and to indicate land spirits, house spirits, and similar beings.

21. This incident is referenced as well in the Lokasenna although there Loki accuses Frigga of infidelity for sleeping with Odin's brothers.

22. There is an ongoing and likely endless debate about the possible connection and even conflation of Frigga and Freya. Evidence is not strong enough to support either arguing successfully for or against the idea. It is beyond the purview of this book to discuss in depth but I will quote Grundy's article 'Freya and Frigga' here: "the problem of whether Frigg or Freyja may have been a single goddess originally is a difficult one, made more so by the scantiness of pre-Viking Age references to Germanic goddesses, and the diverse quality of the sources. The best that can be done is to survey the arguments for and against their identity, and to see how well each can be supported."

23. Generally believed to be Loki in disguise.

24. There are some who speculate that Gefjon may be a name for Freya, making the goddesses identical which could be reinforced by this story, however, she is generally treated as a distinct being in modern Heathenry.

25. Any interpretation of Norse deities through a classical lens should always in my opinion be taken loosely and symbolically, not literally.

26. This was a punishment at the time for unfaithful wives and as in the Lokasenna Loki accuses Sif of infidelity with

himself there has been speculation that he cut off her hair to publicly shame her for this infidelity.

27. You can find a full list of Odin's names and their meanings in my book Pagan Portals - Odin.

28. In alternate version with Hoenir and Lodurr, who may or may not be synonymous with the brothers named here.

29. The folklore for who leads the Wild Hunt varies by area, and while Odin leads it in some places and stories in others the leader may be different, varying from other deities to folkloric figures to famous dead humans.

30. Snorri claims that Sokkvabekkr is Sága's abode however, Grimnismal assigns it to both Odin and Sága, so it may be viewed either way.

31. To be fair, Loki makes this same accusation against several of the goddesses including Tyr's wife who doesn't even appear by name in the account but who Loki claims to have fathered a son on, so either claiming he has slept with the various goddesses is simply a repeating pattern or else Loki had indeed slept with them, perhaps as part of older stories that are now lost.

32. Not to be confused with the similarly named son of Loki or the figure named among the list of dwarves.

33. Worth noting that this is the same female Jotun that gives several items to Thor to aid him. I might suggest that Griðr's magnanimity towards Thor is possibly rooted in her connection to Odin.

34. A reference to the fact that Vidar will kill Fenrir by standing on his lower jaw and pushing his upper jaw until it breaks.

35. Mardoll is a word without a clear meaning but according to Simek is used often as a kenning for gold.

36. The name is uncertain but Simek suggests may possibly be read as 'necklace of lights' and may relate to the aurora borealis.

37. A legal term for a person who was placed outside society for a crime.
38. Alternately to Niflheim depending on the version.
39. Based on the linguistic similarity in the names and lack of overlap in their cults. Simek suggests that Nerthus may have been the predecessor of Njorð who was either first envisioned as female then as male or may have been a hermaphroditic deity.
40. For my own opinion I think this is likely referencing the Ljósálfar whose realm would seem by descriptions to be close to the realm of the Aesir, however, as far as I know the original text does not specify which álfar.
41. the idea of some dead joining the elves after death is something we see as well in the Irish, indicating that this may be a wider concept.
42. See the section on seidhr in the chapter on magic for a better understanding of this concept.
43. A fetch or fjylga is a spirit attached to a human or projected from a human that may act independently from that human or at the person's direction.
44. Wind-elf and wand-elf respectively.
45. Thurs is a term for a dangerous kind of Jotun.
46. Please not there are other forms of kobolds besides just the domestic ones, so that not all kobolds are considered house spirits but the house spirit kind are simply called kobolds.
47. i.e. dwarves.
48. Literally 'Mrs Odin'.
49. The Orkney version of trolls.

Bibliography

Adalsteinsson, J., (1999) Under the Cloak: a Pagan Ritual Turning Point in the Conversion of Iceland

— (1998) A Piece of Horse Liver: Myth, Ritual and Folklore in Old Icelandic Sources

Adam of Bremen (1876) Gesta Hammaburgensis ecclesiae pontificum

American Heritage Dictionary (n.d.) https://www.ahdictionary.com/word/indoeurop.html

Arnold, M., (2011) Thor: Myth to Marvel

Ashliman, D., (2010) Folklore and Mythology Electronic Texts. Retrieved from https://www.pitt.edu/~dash/folktexts.html

Barrett, J., (2008) "The Norse in Scotland"; The Viking World

Bauschatz, P., (1982) The Well and the Tree

Bellows, H., (Trans.) (1936) The Poetic Edda

Berk, A., and Spytma, W., (2002) Penance, Power, and Pursuit, On the Trail of the Wild Hunt

Birley, A., (1999) Agricola and Germany

Blain, J., (2002) Nine Worlds of Seid-Magic

Bray, O., (1908) The Elder or Poetic Edda, commonly known as Sæmund's Edda, part I: The Mythological Poems

Brodeur, A., (1916) The Prose Edda

Byock, J., (1998) The Saga of King Hrolf Kraki

— (2005). The Prose Edda

Cameron, M., (1993) Anglo-Saxon Medicine.

Carmichael, A., (1900) Carmina Gadelica volume 2

Chisholm, J., (2002) Grove and Gallows

Clements, J., (2005) The Vikings

Cook, R., (2001) Njal's Saga

Colm (2013) Thor's Wood, A Sacred Grove Near Viking Age Dublin? Retrieved from irisharchaeology.ie/2013/07/thors-wood-a-sacred-grove-in-viking-dublin/

Coulter, J., (2003) Germanic Heathenry A Practical Guide

Crawford, B., (1987) Scandinavian Scotland

Crossley-Holland, K., (1981) The Norse Myths

Dasent, G., (2001) Popular Tales From Norse Mythology

D'Aulaires, I., and D'Aulaires E., (1967) D'Aulaires' Book of Norse Myths

Downham, C., (2007) Viking Kings of Britain and Ireland: The Dynasty of Ívarr to A.D. 1014

Dumézil, G., (1973) Gods of the Ancient Northmen

Ellis, H., (1968) The Road to Hel

Ellis-Davidson, H., (1964) Gods and Myths of Northern Europe

— (1973) "Hostile Magic in the Icelandic Sagas." In: The Witch Figure: Folklore Essays by a Group of Scholars in England Honouring the 75th Birthday of Katharine M. Briggs

— (1988) Myths and Symbols in Pagan Europe

— (1993) The Lost Beliefs of Northern Europe

Evans, D., (2005) Matronae. Retrieved from http://www.celtnet.org.uk/gods_m/matronae.html

Ewing, T., (2008) Gods and Worshippers in the Viking and Germanic World

Faulkes, A., (1995) Prose Edda

Fischer, L., (2012) Evidence of Vikings by County. Retrieved from http://www.vikingage.mic.ul.ie/resource_vikings-by-county.html

Fisher, P., (1980) Saxo Grammaticus: The History of the Danes Books I-IX

Medievalists (2021) 5 Magic Spells from Medieval Iceland. Retrieved from https://www.medievalists.net/2019/01/5-magic-spells-from-medieval-iceland/

Ford, D., (2001) Royal Berkshire History: Beware the Ghostly Hunt

Fortson, B., (2004) Indo-European language and culture: an introduction

Fulk, R., (2012) *Sigvatr Þórðarson, Austrfararvísur* in Poetry from the Kings' Sagas 1: From Mythical Times to c. 1035

Green, M., (1992) Dictionary of Celtic Myth and Legend

Grimm, J., (1888) Teutonic Mythology, volume 1

— (1966) Teutonic Mythology, volume 2

— (1883) Teutonic Mythology volume 3

Gruber, B., (2007) Iceland: Searching for Elves and Hidden People

Grundy, S., (1995) The Cult of Odinn: God of Death?

— (1994) Miscellaneous Studies Towards the Cult of Odinn

— (1998) *"Freyja and Frigg"*. The Concept of the Goddess

Guðmundsson, O., (2016) Sex in the Sagas: Love and Lust in the Old Icelandic Literature

Gundarsson, K., (2006) Our Troth, volume 1

— (2007) Our Troth volume 2

— (2007) Elves, Wights, and Trolls

Harbert, W., (2006) The Germanic Languages

Harper, D., (2021) Online Etymology Dictionary, 'Odin', Retrieved from http://www.etymonline.com/index.php?term=odin

— (2021) Online Etymology Dictionary 'Heathen', Retrieved from https://www.etymonline.com/word/heathen

Heath, C., (2021) Elves, Witches & Gods: Spinning Old Heathen Magic in the Modern Day

Heinrichs, A., (nd). The Search for Identity: A Problem after the conversion

Herbert, K., (1995)Looking for the Lost Gods of England

Hodge, W., (n.d.) Waelburga and the Rites of May. Retrieved from http://www.friggasweb.org/walburga.html

Hødnebø, Finn, (1987) Who were the first Vikings? Proceedings of the Tenth Viking Congress, Larkollen, Norway 1985

Hollander, L., (1936) Old Norse Poems: The Most Important Nonskaldic Verse Not Included in the Poetic Edda

— (Trans.) (1964) Heimskringla

Hrafnagaldr Óðins https://notendur.hi.is/eybjorn/ugm/hrg/
hrg.html

Hyllested, A., (2010) The Precursors of Celtic and Germanic

Jolly, K., (1996) Popular Religion in Late Saxon England

Jones, M., (2003) The Wild Hunt. Retrieved from www.
maryjones.us/jce/wildhunt.html

Kershaw, K., (2000) The One-eyed God: Odin and the (Indo-)
Germanic Mannerbunde

Lafayllve, P., (2013) A Practical Heathen's Guide to Asatru

Larrington, C., (1996) The Poetic Edda

Lawless, S., (2010) The Ethics of Malevolence. Retrieved
from https://web.archive.org/web/20141021064543/
http://sarahannelawless.com/2010/11/17/the-ethics-of-
malevolence

Lecouteux, C., (1995) Demons and Spirits of the Land

— (1999) Phantom Armies of the Night

— (2000) The Tradition of Household Spirits: Ancestral Lore
and Practices

— (2013) The Hidden History of Elves and Dwarfs: Avatars of
Invisible Realms

Lendering, J., (2013) Matres, Matronae, or Mothers. Retrieved
from http://www.livius.org/man-md/matronae/matronae.
html

Lindow, J., (2001) Norse Mythology A Guide to the Gods,
Heroes, Rituals, and Beliefs

Lockey, N., (1882) Nature, vol. 26

Magoun, F., (1949) 'On the Old-Germanic Altar or Oath Ring';
Acta Philogica Scandinavica

McNeill, F., (1961) The Silver Bough, volume 3

O'Donoghue, H., (2008) From Asgard to Valhalla

Óðins nöfn (n.d.) Skaldic Poetry of the Scandinavian Middle
Ages http://skaldic.abdn.ac.uk/

Orchard, A., (1997) Dictionary of Norse Myth and Legend

Pálsson, H., and Edwards, P., (1981) Orkneyinga Saga

Paxson, D., (2005) Taking Up the Runes

— (2006) Essential Asatru

— (2008) Trance-Portation

Pennick, N., (1993) Runic Magic: the history and practice of ancient runic traditions

Pollington, S., (2003) The Mead-Hall: Feasting in Anglo-Saxon England

Reppion, J., (2016) Spirits of Place

Ross, A., (1998) Pagan Celts

Rowsell, T., (2012) Woden and His Roles in Anglo-Saxon Royal Genealogy

Samuel, S., (2017) 'What To Do When Racists Try To Hijack Your Religion', the Atlantic. Retrieved from https://www.theatlantic.com/international/archive/2017/11/asatru-heathenry-racism/543864/

Scherker, A., (2013) Protecting Elves from Highway Construction is a Thing in Iceland

Schreiwer, R., (2013) The 12 Nights of Wonnetdanz. Retrieved from http://urglaawe.blogspot.com/2013/04/twelve-nights-of-wonnetdanz.html

Scudder, B., (1997) Egil's Saga

Sigrdrifumal (n.d.) Retrieved from http://www.northvegr.org/the%20eddas/the%20poetic%20edda%20%20-%20thorpe%20translation/sigrdrifumal%20-%20the%20lay%20of%20sigrdrifa%20page%201.html

Sigurdsson, G., (2000) Gaelic Influences in Iceland

Simek, R., (1993) Dictionary of Northern Mythology

Simpson, J., (1973) "Olaf Tryggvason versus the Powers of Darkness." In: The Witch Figure: Folklore Essays by a Group of Scholars in England Honouring the 75th Birthday of Katharine M. Briggs

Tacitus (nd) Germania Retrieved from http://www.ourcivilisation.com/smartboard/shop/tacitusc/germany/chap1.htm

Thorpe, B., (1851) Northern Mythology, Compromising the Principal Traditions and Superstitions of Scandinavia, North Germany, and the Netherlands

Turville-Petre, E., (1964) Myth and Religion of the North

Towrie, S., (2013) The Wild Hunt

Vafþrúðnismál (n. d.) Retrieved from http://www.northvegr. org/the%20eddas/the%20poetic%20edda%20%20-%20 thorpe%20translation/vaf%C3%9Er%C3%BA%C3%B0n ism%C3%A1l%20-%20the%20lay%20of%20vafthrudnir. html

Wallis, F., (1999) Bede: The Reckoning of Time

Ward, C., (2012) Vikings in Ireland. Retrieved from http:// www.vikinganswerlady.com/Ireland.shtml

— (2021) Courtship, Love and Marriage in Viking Scandinavia. Retrieved from http://www.vikinganswerlady.com/ wedding.shtml

Wodening, S., (2003) Hammer of the Gods Anglo-Saxon Paganism in Modern Times

World's Strangest (2011) The Mystical Farting Runes of Iceland. Retrieved from http://www.worldsstrangest.com/ mental-floss/the-mystical-farting-runes-of-iceland/

Young, J, (1964) Prose Edda

MOON
BOOKS

PAGANISM & SHAMANISM

What is Paganism? A religion, a spirituality, an alternative belief system, nature worship? You can find support for all these definitions (and many more) in dictionaries, encyclopaedias, and text books of religion, but subscribe to any one and the truth will evade you. Above all Paganism is a creative pursuit, an encounter with reality, an exploration of meaning and an expression of the soul. Druids, Heathens, Wiccans and others, all contribute their insights and literary riches to the Pagan tradition. Moon Books invites you to begin or to deepen your own encounter, right here, right now.

If you have enjoyed this book, why not tell other readers by posting a review on your preferred book site.

Recent bestsellers from Moon Books are:

Journey to the Dark Goddess
How to Return to Your Soul
Jane Meredith
Discover the powerful secrets of the Dark Goddess and
transform your depression, grief and pain into healing
and integration.
Paperback: 978-1-84694-677-6 ebook: 978-1-78099-223-5

Shamanic Reiki
Expanded Ways of Working with Universal Life Force Energy
Llyn Roberts, Robert Levy
Shamanism and Reiki are each powerful ways of healing; together,
their power multiplies. *Shamanic Reiki* introduces techniques to
help healers and Reiki practitioners tap ancient healing wisdom.
Paperback: 978-1-84694-037-8 ebook: 978-1-84694-650-9

Pagan Portals – The Awen Alone
Walking the Path of the Solitary Druid
Joanna van der Hoeven
An introductory guide for the solitary Druid, *The Awen Alone* will
accompany you as you explore, and seek out your own place
within the natural world.
Paperback: 978-1-78279-547-6 ebook: 978-1-78279-546-9

A Kitchen Witch's World of Magical Herbs & Plants
Rachel Patterson
A journey into the magical world of herbs and plants, filled with
magical uses, folklore, history and practical magic. By popular
writer, blogger and kitchen witch, Tansy Firedragon.
Paperback: 978-1-78279-621-3 ebook: 978-1-78279-620-6

Medicine for the Soul
The Complete Book of Shamanic Healing
Ross Heaven
All you will ever need to know about shamanic healing and how to
become your own shaman...
Paperback: 978-1-78099-419-2 ebook: 978-1-78099-420-8

Shaman Pathways – The Druid Shaman
Exploring the Celtic Otherworld
Danu Forest
A practical guide to Celtic shamanism with exercises and
techniques as well as traditional lore for exploring the Celtic
Otherworld.
Paperback: 978-1-78099-615-8 ebook: 978-1-78099-616-5

Traditional Witchcraft for the Woods and Forests
A Witch's Guide to the Woodland with Guided Meditations and
Pathworking
Mélusine Draco
A Witch's guide to walking alone in the woods, with guided
meditations and pathworking.
Paperback: 978-1-84694-803-9 ebook: 978-1-84694-804-6

Wild Earth, Wild Soul
A Manual for an Ecstatic Culture
Bill Pfeiffer
Imagine a nature-based culture so alive and so connected,
spreading like wildfire. This book is the first flame...
Paperback: 978-1-78099-187-0 ebook: 978-1-78099-188-7

Naming the Goddess
Trevor Greenfield
Naming the Goddess is written by over eighty adherents and
scholars of Goddess and Goddess Spirituality.
Paperback: 978-1-78279-476-9 ebook: 978-1-78279-475-2

Shapeshifting into Higher Consciousness
Heal and Transform Yourself and Our World with Ancient
Shamanic and Modern Methods
Llyn Roberts
Ancient and modern methods that you can use every day to
transform yourself and make a positive difference in the world.
Paperback: 978-1-84694-843-5 ebook: 978-1-84694-844-2

Readers of ebooks can buy or view any of these bestsellers by
clicking on the live link in the title. Most titles are published in
paperback and as an ebook. Paperbacks are available in traditional
bookshops. Both print and ebook formats are available online.

Find more titles and sign up to our readers' newsletter at
http://www.johnhuntpublishing.com/paganism
Follow us on Facebook at https://www.facebook.com/MoonBooks
and Twitter at https://twitter.com/MoonBooksJHP